# The Lord's Day

Dr. James P. Wesberry, Executive Director
THE LORD'S DAY ALLIANCE OF THE
UNITED STATES
Suite 107-2930 Flowers Road, South
Atlanta, Georgia 30341

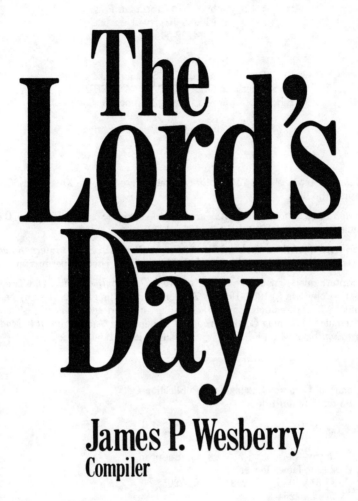

# The Lord's Day

### James P. Wesberry
**Compiler**

BROADMAN PRESS
Nashville, Tennessee

© Copyright 1986 ● Broadman Press
All Rights Reserved
4222-64

ISBN: 0-8054-2264-1
Dewey Decimal Classification: 263.4
Subject Headings: SUNDAY//WORSHIP
Library of Congress Catalog Number: 85-29055

Printed in the United States of America

**Library of Congress Cataloging-in-Publication Data**
Main entry under title:

The Lord's day.

1. Sunday—Sermons.  2. Sermons, American.
I. Wesberry, James Pickett.
BV113.L67  1986      263      85-29055
ISBN 0-8054-2264-1

Lovingly and gratefully dedicated
to my wife
Margaret Spratlin Wesberry,
to my son,
James P. Wesberry, Jr.,
and to
my six grandchildren

# Contents

# Foreword
by Norman Vincent Peale

Since the desecration of the sabbath has progressively developed, this book, *The Lord's Day*, brings a much-needed message.

Many of us fondly remember the American "sabbath" that existed from the founding of the republic until just a few years ago. Something inexpressibly precious is lost to Americans with the secularization of Sunday.

An old hymn describes the Lord's Day "O Day of Rest and Gladness." The Lord's Day Alliance of the United States, under the inspired leadership of Dr. James P. Wesberry, executive director, has valiantly striven to preserve the values of the time-honored and historic American sabbath, the Lord's Day. The publication of this fascinating book, to which distinguished writers have contributed, will do much to recover and preserve for us and for our children our great Lord's Day heritage.

*Norman Vincent Peale*

# Introduction

by James P. Wesberry

One of the first things I attempted to do when I became executive director of the Lord's Day Alliance of the United States, some ten years ago, was to secure a good bibliography dealing with the Lord's Day. I found some wonderful books that have influenced me, but I felt then, as I do now, that there is a shortage of such books.

Paul Butler, author of the Best Sermon Series, was a good friend of mine. I once asked him how many sermons he had received dealing with the Christian sabbath. If my memory serves me correctly, he said none. As I searched through his books I did find one, and it was a really good one by Dr. Leslie Weatherhead. There may have been others.

I have had many ministers ask me where they might find material to help them preach on this subject. I have been able to recommend some good books, and now I am happy to add another which to me is a gold mine of such material. It should be helpful not only to ministers but to all people who are interested in the Lord's Day, and especially laypersons.

This book is different from most of the books I have seen or read. The Lord's Day Alliance of the United States and its affiliate, The Lord's Day League of New England, are almost one-hundred years old. We will soon be celebrating the one-hundredth birthday of The Lord's Day Alliance. It is most timely that we should select some of the outstanding sermons and addresses delivered to their members and others, and present them to our friends upon the eve of our centennial.

I acknowledge my deep indebtedness to my good friend, Dr. Norman Vincent Peale, pastor of Marble Collegiate Church, New York City, and editor of *Guideposts*, who with Mrs. Peale has been a highly treasured member of the board of managers of The Lord's Day Alliance for many years, for writing the foreword and for allowing us to use one of his messages which appeared in *Guideposts* some time ago entitled, "Something Infinitely Precious." Both Dr. and Mrs. Peale have been a great and constant source of inspiration and encouragement to us in our work of preserving the Lord's Day in America. They have helped set the pace for sabbath observance in America. They have never failed to answer our calls. I am profoundly grateful to the Fleming H. Revell Company of Old Tappan, New Jersey, for permission to use the message, "One Day in Seven," from the book, *Be an Extraordinary Person in an Ordinary World,* authored by Dr. Robert H. Schuller and edited by his son Dr. Robert A. Schuller, an honored member of the board of managers of The Lord's Day Alliance of the United States.

I also wish to thank my good friend, Dr. Wyeth Willard, of Forestdale, Massachusetts, president of the Lord's Day League of New England, for permission to use the messages by Dr. E. Stanley Jones and Dr. Frederick Brown Harris, former chaplain of the United States Senate. All messages are used by permission.

Two of the messages are by outstanding laypersons— one, S. Truett Cathy, president and owner of Chick-fil-A of Atlanta, who has greatly encouraged this book; the other by one of Atlanta's outstanding men in public relations, Hugh Cates. I am honored to present two personal

messages, "Preserving Our Liberty Through the Observance of the Lord's Day," and "Perplexing Questions
About the Lord's Day."

This will be my fourth book by Broadman Press, and I
wish very much to express my deepest and most sincere
appreciation to my friends at Broadman Press who have
been so kind to me. I thank Mrs. Mildred Shockley for
typing my manuscript, each contributor, and especially
my administrative associate, "Miss Margaret," who has
also served as my secretary for over forty years and is now
Mrs. Wesberry.

It is my humble prayer that as The Lord's Day Alliance
of the United States completes its first century of service
in 1988 and enters into its second century in this ever-
changing, complex age, that this book on the Lord's Day
will give inspiration, strength, and guidance to many who
love the Lord and His Day.

Whatever royalty comes from this book will go to the
Sue Latimer Wesberry Memorial Fund to promote the
work of The Lord's Day Alliance in seeking to preserve
the Lord's Day in America.

*James P. Wesberry*
*Atlanta, Georgia*

# 1
# Preserving Our Liberty by Observing the Lord's Day

*Leviticus 25:10*

by James P. Wesberry

On the walls of the Smithsonian Institute are these words: "To secure the blessings of liberty for posterity is the goal of the American Republic."

One of the most beautiful, thrilling, and no doubt providential events in American history took place when our forefathers were about to land at Plymouth Rock. One of the main reasons why they left England for refuge in Holland, fled from Holland back to England, and finally went from Southhampton to the Western wilderness was their love for liberty and the sabbath. King James had ruled by law that the sabbath should be a day of games and pleasure.

The early Pilgrims thought this was wrong and braved untold hardships of sixty-three stormy days on the rough Atlantic that they might have a sabbath of their own choosing. They were determined to build this nation upon the foundation and superstructure of liberty and the sabbath.

As they were about to land at Plymouth Rock, something miraculous happened, something that profoundly influenced the future of American life. It helped to mold and make the character of the American nation. It is the key that unlocks the door of the first century, at least, of our nation's history of the keeping of the sabbath.

Imagine their excitement and joy! After a long and ter-

rible voyage they were now about to land. It was Saturday. But a strange thing happened. Suddenly a storm
arose and drove them to the shore of Clark Island where
they disembarked and made shelter for the night.

The next day was Sunday. Instead of reloading their
ships and sailing for Plymouth Rock, they spent that day
in prayer, praise, thanksgiving, and worship of Almighty
God. On Monday, December 11, 1620, the Pilgrims set
sail and landed at Plymouth Rock.

The Pilgrims had deep convictions about the Lord's
Day. They did not leave these convictions behind them in
England or Holland. They brought their love and loyalty
for the Christian sabbath and their devotion to liberty
with them. Nor did their courage fail them. We should
never cease to be grateful to God for them and all others
who have given us such a rich and glorious heritage.

On July 4, 1976, we celebrated the two-hundredth
birthday of our nation. What a day it was! Liberty bells
and church bells sounded everywhere. It was a time of
great joy. We had something to rejoice about. And it
seemed most significant that it came on Sunday. Surely
that, too, was providential, as if to say, Sunday is at the
very heart of our nation, and we couldn't have survived
two hundred years without it. The French infidel Voltaire
is reputed to have once said that Christianity could never
be destroyed as long as the weekly sabbath remained. The
Christian sabbath may well be called the chief symbol of
Christianity because the resurrection of Jesus Christ from
the grave is the chief cornerstone of the Christian temple.
The Christian sabbath is a memorial of that.

I have tried to imagine what it was like in America some
two hundred years ago. Our nation was torn and divided
between a desire for peace, stability, and abiding unity
with our mother country and the wish to be free. Out of
the turmoil and strife of those difficult times emerged the

immortal Declaration of Independence, a flaming torch which sheds "freedom's holy light" not only over the United States but also over the whole world.

I don't think I have ever appreciated the liberty we enjoy here in the United States more than when our ship landed early one morning in Leningrad. The ship was the *Bergensfjord.* I was the Protestant chaplain on this ship for a forty-one-day trip to the Land of the Midnight Sun and to Russia. There were no brass bands to greet us, no smiling children waving us a welcome, no crowd to greet us, there was nothing but solemn silence and some gloomy-looking Russian soldiers who examined our passports. Many of our passengers did not care to disembark, and remained on ship. We spent three days sightseeing in Leningrad and Moscow.

We were afraid to talk above a whisper in our hotel rooms for fear they might be "bugged". The beautiful churches had been turned into museums. The Bibles, pulpits, great religious art, and various treasures from the churches were now in museums. Religion was something of the past. Russia was engaged in a struggle against God. Bibles and other religious books were available only on the black market. A handful of churches, open in spite of Communism, were owned and operated by the government. We could not find a church of any kind. Our guide had never heard of a Baptist church. A Roman Catholic priest with us could not find a Catholic church. How sad and tragic!

As we were about to leave Moscow my wife looked out of the car window and suddenly exclaimed, "What a beautiful rainbow!" And we all saw a pretty rainbow overarching the heavens. It seemed to say something to me. "Rainbow over Russia!" I thought, *Is this not God's promise that someday He will come back to His throne in Russia? And someday the Russian people will say, "We*

*are tired of being robbed of our God," and will cry out for
Him. They will say, "Give us God," and there will be a
great spiritual awakening throughout all their great nation and people will come to know and love and serve the
God they have forsaken.* When I returned home I wrote
a series of articles on Russia, put them in a little book, and
entitled it, *Rainbow Over Russia.* It went like hotcakes.
That was in 1962.

Then, in 1975 my wife and I returned to Moscow. This
time we were determined to see the First Baptist Church
there which was one of the few churches allowed to remain open. We had the address written down. One afternoon we went out in front of our large hotel to try to get
a taxi to take us there. We showed several cab drivers a
slip of paper with the address and one of them made the
sign of the cross and said "Baptist" and we replied by
nodding. We got in his cab and away we went. It seemed
about twelve miles from our hotel. We were going to take
a picture of the church and hurry back to the hotel to
rejoin our party. But God had other plans for us.

A deacon whose face shone like an angel's came out
and, speaking English, asked us to dismiss our taxi, saying
he would get us another one. He invited us to meet the
pastor and his associates and see what was happening.
They had worship there almost every night, he said. The
church was full upstairs and down. We had a very enjoy-
able visit with the pastor who graciously welcomed us. We
were given an interpreter and seats in the balcony. The
church was so overcrowded that there were people standing in the aisle.

The music began. It was soft and beautiful. The choir
came in, followed by the ministers. The singing was inspiring. The pastor prayed and I could feel the presence
of God. The power of the Holy Spirit was there. The
audience consisted mostly of elderly people. As the pastor

prayed some of them wiped tears from their eyes, and I, too, wept. I was reminded of how when I was a boy Woodrow Wilson was President of the United States, and one day his secretary came in and found him weeping and asked him why. He replied, "I am weeping for the imperiled liberties of the world." I thought of Jesus weeping over Jerusalem. And as I wiped tears from my eyes and cheeks, I said: "O, my God, if I ever write another book about Russia, it won't be on *Rainbow Over Russia* but it will be on *Tears Over Russia.*

There is much to weep about. As I thought about the imperiled liberties of multiplied millions of Russians and of other people of the world, I thanked God for the privilege of being an American citizen.

If you really want something to weep about, then weep over what is happening to the American sabbath, weep over the ever-increasing disrespect, decay, deterioration, and desecration of the Lord's Day.

My phone rang in Atlanta one morning, and when I said hello, a preacher friend said, "My heart is broken. I am sitting here weeping over what you wrote in *Sunday* magazine about those preachers in Texas who closed their churches in order that their people might attend a Super Bowl football game." The money lovers and pleasure seekers would steal the Holy Sabbath inch by inch. It's good to know that somebody cares enough to weep over it.

In Moscow, I went to the Kremlin in Red Square and saw nearby the great Tsar Bell. It literally dwarfs you. It originally weighed two-hundred tons and was cast by a father and son in the eighteenth century. It was placed in preparatory stage on a scaffold in the Kremlin but fell into a pit of water and cracked. The cracked piece weighs eleven-and-one-half tons. It took five years to mold it. One-hundred years later it was taken out of the pit and

installed on a granite base in the Kremlin. It is known as
the bell that never rang—the bell that never made a
sound. What a pity! A bell made to ring that never rings.
A soundless bell!

What a tragedy to be made to speak and to remain
silent! Oh, the awful tragedy of silence! When we hold our
silences, the very stones cry out against us. When good
men are silent, evil flourishes. Why all the reticence concerning the importance of the Lord's Day and its proper
observance? Why don't our ministers speak out more
loudly and clearly on this subject? Why do they have such
a strange case of laryngitis?

Paul Butler was the author of a large number of
volumes of the *Best Sermon Series,* a dozen or more, I
think. He invited ministers to submit sermons on any and
all subjects. He received some fifteen thousand or more
sermons from which he selected what he considered to be
the best. I once asked him, "How many sermons have you
had submitted concerning the importance of the Sabbath
Day?" I was amazed at his reply. "None," he said. This is
unbelievable. Later I did find one sermon along this line
in one of his books. But, why all this silence?

It reminds me of what my good friend Martin Niemoeller once said. My wife and I went to Princeton one summer largely because Niemoeller was there. We sat at his
feet and heard his marvelous gospel messages. When the
conference was over, we changed our plans in order to
drive Dr. and Mrs. Niemoeller to New York City. We
enjoyed several wonderful hours with them. I can see
them now as they waved us good-bye. Mrs. Niemoeller
died some years ago, and Dr. Niemoeller died in March,
1984, at Wiesbaden at the age of ninety-two. He had spent
eight years in a Nazi concentration camp for leading opposition to Adolph Hitler. He had been a submarine com-
mander during the First World War and a great hero. He

was a powerful Lutheran preacher. He served as president of the World Council of Churches in 1961-1963. He received the Lenin Peace Prize in 1962 and the Grand Cross of Merit, West Germany's medal of highest honor, in 1971.

Niemoller said,

> In Germany they came first for the Communists, and I didn't speak up because I wasn't a Communist. Then they came for the Jews, and I didn't speak up because I wasn't a Jew. Then they came for the trade unionists, and I didn't speak up because I wasn't a trade unionist. Then they came for the Catholics, and I didn't speak up because I was a Protestant. Then they came for me and by that time no one was left to speak up.

And this is how it is. If we say nothing, if we remain silent, the time may come when there will be nobody to speak up.

Then I went to Philadelphia and stood before the Liberty Bell. I had been there before. The Liberty Bell was made by Thomas Lester at Whiteford Foundry in London and arrived in Philadelphia in 1752 inscribed with the biblical quotation from Leviticus: "Proclaim liberty throughout all the land unto all the inhabitants thereof" (Lev. 25:10). It was cracked at the first stroke and recast twice. It was rung on important occasions and especially in connection with the signing of the Declaration of Independence. In 1935 it was cracked permanently and, since then, has had to be tapped cautiously with a soft rubber mallet.

One day a distinguished Chinese visitor stood before the Liberty Bell and looked at the crack and asked, "Is American liberty cracked?" Some of us have asked this same question. Is liberty cracked? The answer is yes, there are cracks! And a crack may be a serious, ominous, costly thing. It is a danger signal—a warning. A crack is a forewarning of calamity. Think of what a crack might mean in the ceiling of any building. Cracks must be repaired. Enemies may creep through the cracks from the outside to undermine and destroy us. It is therefore of utmost importance that we repair these cracks.

The old Statue of Liberty which has stood in New York harbor holding aloft the torch of freedom is crying for help. It was dedicated in 1886. In 1986, it will be one-hundred years old. The statue's right hand and the torch it holds are badly corroded. President Reagan has asked Americans to join in a tremendous national effort to rescue her and to rededicate the nation to the traditional values she represents. The president has encouraged people to give $230 million to restore it, which will take one to two years. At this writing is now closed for repairs, scheduled to reopen in 1986.

We must do some repair work on the Statue of Liberty —and we must also do some repair work on the values it represents—liberty and the Lord's Day. They are twins. If you lose one, you lose the other. As you guard one, you guard the other. Our text, "Proclaim liberty throughout all the land unto all the inhabitants thereof," tells us how close they are to each other. In Exodus, God commands us to keep one day out of seven holy. In Leviticus, God says the land must have a sabbath, and that there must be a sabbath every seven years and the fiftieth year shall be a year of jubilee—and liberty shall be proclaimed "throughout all the land unto all the inhabitants thereof."

Liberty is every person's birthright. The standard of liberty unfurled in Philadelphia in 1776 was not the first to gladden human hearts. History tells of many others who rose to throw off the yoke of oppression and to declare themselves independent, only to lose their independence for lack of eternal vigilance. Rome did. Rome paid the price but forgot and thus lost her highest prize. And this has been true of many other kingdoms, empires, and countries.

We love our country, its flag—the old red, white, and blue. We love its people, its freedom, the Declaration of Independence, our immortal Constitution, and the Bill of Rights. Our liberty was bought at a great price—the price of blood. But to be preserved we must have the highest type of patriotism. To preserve our liberty and these valuable documents we must be a God-loving, God-fearing, God-honoring people. To secure constitutional government we need that pause with our week's occupation in the quiet peaceful hours of the Lord's Day. One day's rest and worship in seven makes us better citizens. It is the Sunday-cultivated character we need to give us a citizen body and an electorate fit to guard and preserve our liberty.

This is what The Lord's Day Alliance is all about. In 1888, almost a hundred years ago, a national sabbath organization was formed to preserve this priceless heritage. Representatives of several denominations met in the Foundry Methodist Church in Washington, D. C., December 11-12, and The American Sabbath Union was organized. The name was later changed to The Lord's Day Alliance of the United States.

For all these years The Lord's Day Alliance has been a powerful force, the only national organization according to our knowledge, the sole purpose of which is to preserve the Lord's Day in America. The Lord's Day Alliance seeks to preserve this most treasured of traditional values in the highest attainment in religion and morale upon which the stability and well-being of our nation depend.

Composed of representatives of twenty-three denominations on its board of managers, The Lord's Day Alliance helps to keep alive an awareness of the Lord's Day and the importance of keeping it as "unto the Lord." It serves as a guardian of Sunday and a safeguard of a common day of rest for all people. It serves as a right arm to pastors and churches in urging people to keep the sabbath day holy and to use it as a day of rest, worship, spiritual instruction and renewal, family culture, and service to others. If America is great, it is great not only because of its great preachers and churches, but because it has not forgotten to keep the sabbath day.

The Lord's Day Alliance is dedicated to the fulfillment of the purpose for which it was created, namely: "To promote the first day of the week, the Lord's Day, as the Christian day of renewal and worship according the Scriptures and for that purpose to gather and diffuse information, to publish documents, to use the press, to cause public addresses to be made and to use other means as shall be expedient to the end that the blessings of the Lord's Day shall be secured for all people."

We declare ourselves unapologetically against the adverse influences arising from business and pleasure, both of which so strongly assert themselves and threaten the integrity of this blessed day of worship, rest, and family culture.

In the words of our beloved and distinguished president, Charles A. Platt, "We are not so much concerned about laws that restrict action in a free society as we are in promoting the benefits accruing from a day of worship and rest each week." In recent years many so-called Blue Laws have been declared unconstitutional. There are about twenty states that still have some kind of Sunday laws. The Lord's Day Alliance is interested in God's laws. From a standpoint of government we are concerned about constitutional laws.

We believe that there should be some kind of protection wrapped around the working man or woman who is compelled to work on his or her chosen sabbath, when to do so is a violation of their religious convictions and their conscience. We strongly support and recommend an amendment to the 1964 Civil Rights Act which would give such a person some relief.

We believe that it is important to get people to the polls to vote but that it is more important to preserve the sabbath day. We believe it is wrong to use the Lord's Day or any part of it for our national Election Day. We think it would be much better for the moral and religious welfare of our nation for our present Election Day of Tuesday to be changed into a national holiday or that we use some other day. For this and many other reasons we strongly oppose the efforts in the Congress to change the Election Day to Sunday.

We also think it is wrong for the owners and managers of shopping malls to require a seven-day lease of their tenants. There might well be some law prohibiting this.

We believe that there is a law above every law and that is God's law. We are anxious to remind all people of this law and of the importance of keeping it. We believe the Lord's Day is the day of our Lord's resurrection from the grave. This is why we celebrate the first day of the week instead of the seventh because Christ rose on the first day—Sunday, and that day should be a great day of rejoicing, a day of delight, a grand, glorious, wonderful, thrilling day, one that is celebrated humbly, gratefully, gladly, joyfully, prayerfully, and reverently.

We believe the time has come when Christians must be Christians. We must return to apostolic living. We must stand up for our convictions, for what we believe. We must keep the Lord's Day because we love the Lord and because we want to honor Him, not because we are forced to do it. It must be a matter of love, a voluntary matter, a matter of conscience.

I am happy to say that there are many like this. We call upon Christians to stand up and be counted, to abstain from shopping on Sunday and, unless their business is one of absolute necessity or mercy, to close on Sunday. We have plenty of outstanding followers of Jesus Christ who do this and who do it because they love Him and not because they are compelled to do it. They are compelled only by that inner love, loyalty, and obedience.

I think of Walter Hoving, chairman of the board of Tiffany's, the famous New York jewelry firm. One morning a few years ago my phone rang and somebody called to ask if I had seen a national television show that morning featuring the chairman of Tiffany's. I had not and was interested. The interviewer had questioned Hoving. There was a sign "We are closed on Sundays." He asked Hoving something like this: "You are big-time jewelers. You say you are closed on Sunday, but suppose someone came along and wanted to buy a half-million-dollar gem on Sunday, you'd sell to him, wouldn't you?"

"I would not," replied Mr. Hoving. "He couldn't get it from Tiffany's on Sunday."

I was so impressed with this story that I phoned Tiffany's in Atlanta and asked for Hoving's phone number in New York. I called him and told him how glad I was to know that we had a man like him in the United States, that I was proud of him and his stand, and thanked him for myself and my board of managers. He was most grateful and gracious. He said, "I'll let you in on a secret. The Lord runs Tiffany's." The Lord runs Tiffany's! I like that. Isn't it great?

The Prince Corporation in the Holland/Zeeland section of Michigan has three plants and employs eight-hundred people. It has grown by leaps and bounds. They manufacture interior auto parts. Their annual sales run over $100 million. The president of the company says:

"We wear our convictions up front. This company has never worked a Sunday in its life. If we run a plant on Sunday, we can't be in church."

The following full-page ad recently appeared in a Spartanburg, South Carolina newspaper: "WE STAND ALONE IN CLOSING ON SUNDAY. A day of rest—a day of worship—a day of togetherness with friends and families—that's what closed on Sundays means to our employees in all 39 areas which we proudly serve. OPEN MONDAY THROUGH SATURDAY. SEE YOU IN CHURCH ON SUNDAY."

Broadus Littlejohn, Jr., a great Christian layman who owns and operates these Community Cash Stores, says that they have always been closed on Sundays and always will be as long as he operates them.

I asked him one day if it cost him money to close his stores on Sunday and he said, "Yes, it cost me one million dollars in one city, but I'll starve before I'll ever open one of my places of business on Sunday or sell alcoholic beverages in them."

I thank God for Coach Vince Dooley of the University of Georgia. Following the strike of the National Football League which removed all of the usual professional football games on Sunday afternoon, one of the major networks contacted Coach Dooley, head coach and director of the University of Georgia football team, and asked him if he would consider the possibility of rescheduling the Georgia games for Sunday afternoon. Coach Dooley replied that, although this would mean a great deal of money and fine national exposure for his team, he would have to turn down the offer, stating that he did not believe that college games should be played on Sunday afternoon.

I thank God for Eric Liddell. All the world knows the thrilling story of the Academy-Award-winning movie *Chariots of Fire*. Representing his native Scotland as a student at the University of Edinburgh in the 1924 Olympics of Paris, Liddell was the favorite to win the gold medal in the one-hundred-meter race. But because the race was set on Sunday, he withdrew. Despite the strongest urging from his countrymen and from friends and relatives, he would not participate. Later in the week he won the gold medal in the four-hundred-meter race, a race he had not been expected to win. He later went to China as a missionary. His life story was written by Sally Magnusson in *The Flying Scotsman.*

And how we admire those two wonderful twins, Richard and Raymond Buker, who while students at Bates College, Lewiston, Maine, were invited by the U.S. Olympic Committee to try out for the 1920 U.S. team. There was a problem, however. The tryouts were to be held on Sunday. Can you believe it? Richard and Raymond both declined to run. He told us when in Atlanta, being honored by The Lord's Day Alliance, that the reason for this was that "when God created the world, He rested upon the seventh day and hallowed it. This has never changed," said Richard, and Raymond nodded his approval.

In 1926 they both went to China as missionaries and spent many years there, Richard serving as a medical missionary and Raymond as a teacher and evangelist. They now live in retirement in Florida. Their thrilling life story may be read in a book entitled *Against the Clock,* by Eric S. Fife.

Another incredible story has to do with one of Atlanta's noblest Christian citizens. Like the story of Eric Liddell, and the Buker twins and others, it is a true story. It really happened. A series of pressures was put on this outstanding Christian businessman to break him down and cause him to change his convictions about keeping one of his places of business open on Sunday.

David Puttnam, who won the Oscar in 1981 for Best

Picture of the Year, told a group of his friends recently that the purpose of *Chariots of Fire* was to portray the supremacy of conscience and ethics over expediency. He was quoted as saying, "The most important scene in the film is the one where the Prince of Wales and the British Olympic Committee attempt to persuade Liddell [the Scottish athlete] to act against his conscience. That is the everyday for each of us—the boardroom, the office, the local committee meeting—where we make our petty compromises with truth and principle."

This is the crux of the whole thing! Imagine it happening every day! Imagine trying to persuade people to go against their conscience, to make petty compromises with truth and principle.

But Eric Liddell was not built that way. Neither was our Atlanta Christian businessman.

Our businessman somehow was permitted to open his business in one of the world's largest malls with permission to close on Sunday. For this he was most grateful. All others opened on Sunday. A million or more people trade at this mall. Many church people say they go there for recreation and to mix and mingle in a nice environment.

Well-dressed people go there directly from church. They eat there. They sit on the nice benches in pleasant garden areas. They park free.

The world has changed from the time we were young, our businessman friend was told. Now, most people, almost all of them, want to use Sunday as a holiday. Mother can get out of the house and not have to cook. To go to a movie or a ball game is very expensive. We are rendering an important public service by being open on Sunday afternoon, said the spokesman of the mall. Our businessman friend heard, "If this does not justify in your mind that it is reasonable and moral for us to open on Sunday, we would like for you to know that we are also concerned about our employees working on Sunday, but they work because they want to and we believe they understand that they are providing a public service.

"We have respect for your principles," our friend was told. "We understand that you desire to permit your people to honor the sabbath and have a day of rest, but we have made a survey which indicates that churchgoers are very happy to have us open Sunday afternoon so they can come here at no cost. You see," the mall spokesman said, "it is appropriate for us to ask people to work on Sunday because we are rendering an essential service, and it is possible that some of the young people who work for you couldn't go to college if they didn't work on Saturday and Sunday and, after all, their Sunday workday does not start until after church.

"We urge you, Mr. Businessman, to open your business Sunday to provide this essential service. The main reason why people eat out on Sunday is so mother and wife can rest and only those employees who volunteer work on Sundays.

"We would be very happy for you to try Sunday afternoon openings for awhile and for you to feel free to revert back to closing if you wish.

"We have a very attractive mall and you have a very attractive business. We have thousands of people, many church people who are being denied the right of doing business with you on Sunday afternoons. They deserve a chance to do business with you instead of looking through a closed window.

"We hope you will give this your deep consideration. We want to make it clear that the economic impact, if you open or stay closed, is absolutely minimal. But, if you feel that the points we have set forth are valid and will consider opening on Sunday, we would like to offer our contribution in the amount of $5,000 to the churches or organization of your choice."

As Eric Liddell refused to run on Sunday, our great Christian businessman thanked the mall official for the privilege of being there and of staying closed on Sunday, and said most magnificently, "You are the kind of person we would like to honor with any reasonable request, but please understand, we cannot compromise on certain principles."

Truett Cathy, president and owner of Chick-Fil-A, Incorporated, tells this story for himself in the chapter entitled "What Sunday Means to Me."

Five Christian girls from Baptist, Methodist, and Roman Catholic backgrounds representing the Hendricks County (Indiana) Gymnastics Team had been practicing for months for the Indiana State Amateur Athletic Union Class 4 Gymnastics Meet in Pendleton, Indiana, until they learned it would be held on Palm Sunday.

They lost their chance to win the Indiana state gymnastics title when they decided to attend church on Palm Sunday instead of competing. Betty Wright, who coaches the girls whose ages range from ten to fourteen, said, "We believe that our talents were given to us by God and we intend to glorify Him with our gifts."

Mrs. Wright brought the problem to the attention of the officials of the amateur athletic union who said they had no control over whether the meet should be held on Palm Sunday.

"We can't praise God and glorify Him if we're missing church on one of the holiest days of the year," the coach said.

"A Company is like a person," says Ronald R. Frost, president of Piggly Wiggly Southern. "It has a system of values. We are profit motivated within certain parameters. But we're not going to do just anything to make a dollar."

Many of the chain stores are open twenty-four hours, seven days a week. That means many of them are open on Sunday. But Piggly Wiggly Southern has bucked that trend. All eighty-two stores are closed on Sunday.

"Many of our employees want that as a day of rest," says Fisher Barfoot, vice-president for marketing. "Hopefully, if we're not requiring them to go to work, they'll go to church."

Piggly Wiggly has also opted not to sell beer and wine.

But there is something more important than doing anything to make a dollar.

On Monday, April 16, 1984, millions of Americans and others throughout the world watched the Boston Marathon on television, the oldest such event with a continued history in existence today. But had it not been for one alert, persistent, believing, and praying pastor, The Reverend Richard A. Germaine, minister for eleven years of the First Congregational Church in Hopkinton, Massachusetts, the 1984 marathon would have been held on Sunday, April 15, instead of Monday.

Dr. Wyeth Willard, president of the Lord's Day League of New England, Incorporated, tells this thrilling story in an article in *Sunday*, Spring 1984 edition, under the title of "The Boston Marathon Did Not Run On Sunday."

On and on I could go with exciting stories of how Christians in every state in the union are believing in, observing, and defending the Lord's Day.

We are told that the celebration of the Lord's Day was so notorious to the heathen in the early days of Christianity that they would ask the martyrs on their way to death, "Do you keep Sunday?" And the martyrs' reply was: "I am a Christian: I cannot omit it." We thank God that we have many great Christian businessmen and women like that today.

The Lord's Day Alliance of the United States has a board of managers consisting of seventy-five godly religious leaders, both men and women, giant leaders of many denominations and states, with a number of auxiliary organizations. The Lord's Day Alliance represents millions of Christians who love the Lord Jesus Christ and His Day and want to see it observed in a way that honors Him.

Some of our friends—the Jews, Seventh-Day Adventists, Seventh-Day Baptists and others—choose Saturday, the seventh day, as their sabbath. The Moslems select Friday beginning at sundown on Thursday. The vast majority of Christians observe the first day of the week as the Lord's Day.

We believe with all of our hearts that all days are God's days and that every day should be lived for God but that Sunday is uniquely His day and should be kept holy. It is not so much a question of what shall we do or what shall we not do on the Lord's Day, but how shall we keep the Lord's Day in a way that honors Christ? Dr. Roy L. Honeycutt, in his book *These Ten Words,* well says: "Rewarding observance of the Commandments seeks to consecrate one day in seven as a symbol of the consecration of all of life and space. The sanctity of one day out of seven symbolizes the sanctity of all life."

We believe that Christians should observe the Lord's Day in a way that honors Christ for many reasons. May I suggest a few?

*Sunday is the Lord's Day!* It is the day of our Lord's resurrection from the grave. Christ rose from the grave on the first day of the week, Sunday, the Lord's Day. The Lord's Day, therefore, should be observed reverently, joyfully, gladly, humbly, and prayerfully.

*Sunday is a holy day* and it should be kept holy. The whole day should be kept holy and not just a part of it. We are not to offer to God half a Lord's Day and then slip into a glorified holiday. It should be wholly dedicated to the Lord, not some of it, but every bit of it.

*Sunday is a day for rest.* In human life, day cannot succeed day without the rhythm of work and sleep. God's very choice of night and day reminds us of this principle of rest. The rhythm of rest and activity is the basis of the laws of nature and people who lay these laws aside do so at their own risk. That's why Sunday is so important. God Himself rested on the sabbath and He wants us to rest.

*Sunday is a day for worship.* In Hebrews 10:25 we are told not to forsake the assembling of ourselves together. This lovely day is given to us as a day for divine worship. It is a day for spiritual growth—a wonderful day for fellowship with God's children in God's house.

*Sunday is a day for special consideration of others.* We are not to be a stumbling block in the way of others who would use this day for rest and worship. Cain asked, "Am I my brother's keeper?" (Gen. 4:9). The answer is, "Yes, you are your brother's keeper; in fact, you are your brother's brother or sister."

*Sunday is the best antidote for boredom in a hurly-burly world.* If we "Remember the sabbath day, to keep it holy" (Ex. 20:8), we will not turn the Lord's Day into a day of pleasure and business as usual. It will be different for us, because as Christians we are different and we will always be mindful that in keeping the sabbath holy we are obeying the law of God—the Fourth Commandment.

*Sunday is a day for family union and reunion.* It is a day for families to get together. Families who pray together and worship together stay together. How beautiful it is for families to be in worship and at the family altar! Sunday should be the happiest day of the week for families.

Take the Bible in your hands and open it. You will find that it begins with the beautiful picture of creation. After God created the heavens and the earth, and all that in six days, we see the beauty of God resting on the seventh day. We see Him walking in harmonious relationship with Adam in the cool of the evening in the Garden of Eden. As we turn the pages of this sacred Book we find the beautiful picture of the last great sabbath, when God has made His new heaven, new earth, and a new sabbath. Again we will rest in perfect harmony between the first and last sabbaths, until God calls us to our eternal sabbath.

One day a father told his little son how, when he had been a boy about his age, he had attended a country church where there was a large bell they used to let him ring. When he had rung the bell, people had come to church in their wagons and buggies and had a wonderful time in worship, in hearing the reading and preaching of God's Word, and in fellowship. He said those were some of the happiest memories of his life. Someday, he told his son, he hoped to take him to see that old country church and the bell.

The little fellow could hardly wait. It was thrilling for him when that day arrived. There was the old church, worn by the ravages of time, with weeds all around. It had been long forsaken. They found their way in and, sure enough, there was the old rope and there was the bell. The little fellow's eyes gleamed. He looked up the rope and at the bell and exclaimed, "Ring it again, Daddy, ring it again!" Once again the old church bell rang and people came from far and wide to see what it was all about.

Let us proclaim loudly and clearly the blessings of liberty and the Lord's Day "throughout all the land unto all the inhabitants thereof."

# 2
# Day of Praise, Joy, and Freedom

*Revelation 1*

by Charles A. Platt

The Fourth Commandment is the most delightful of all the ten to obey.

> Remember the sabbath day, to keep it holy. Six days shalt thou labour, and do all thy work: but the seventh is the sabbath of the Lord thy God; in it thou shalt not do any work, thou, nor thy son, nor thy daughter, thy manservant, nor thy maidservant, nor thy cattle, nor thy stranger that is within thy gates. For in six days the Lord made heaven and earth, the sea and all that in them is, and rested the seventh day. Wherefore the Lord blessed the sabbath day, and hallowed it (Ex. 20:8-11).

We are instructed *not to work,* but to praise God, and to enjoy as much freedom as possible. What a thrill! We share the joy of being alive, unencumbered with most of our responsibilities; then we return to the weekday world refreshed and more enthusiastic than ever. Don't cheat yourself of such a privilege.

It is an old, old religious institution—this sabbath day, or Lord's Day as we Christians like to term it. For more than three thousand years, generations throughout the world have looked to the Ten Commandments as the essence of their moral standards and their relationship to God. That Fourth Commandment begins with the word

*Remember.* It was an old, well-established religious principle even when Moses brought it to the people's attention.

And we Christians have placed strong emphasis on it since the very inception of our faith. Go back to the early days of the church, and picture the plight of John, the disciple, on the Isle of Patmos. Sent to that lonely island in the Mediterranean Sea, off the shipping lanes, sparsely inhabited. So far as John knew, he was doomed to remain there until he died.

The refinements of torture in such a place included both physical suffering and brainwashing. John was alone; probably his only fellow humans were his jailers; and they were under strictest orders to keep their contacts with the prisoner to a minimum.

Why was he there? He tells us in the opening portion of the last book in the Bible: "I John, your brother, who share with you in Jesus the tribulation and the kingdom and the patient endurance, was on the island called Patmos *on account of the Word of God and the testimony of Jesus*" (Rev. 1:9, RSV, Author's italics). It was the easiest way the authorities had of silencing him. They had learned that public executions often fanned the flame of new opposition more than they eliminated dissension.

A person was just sent away; no contact was allowed with him after that. And in his isolation he was the victim of slow sadism. Periodically, according to a schedule prescribed by the authorities, the prisoner's food ration was diminished. Slowly, and in agony, he died of starvation.

John was faced with this sort of existence. We believe a change in government policy, somewhere along the line, effected his release; therefore, we have the account of his religious experience. But he had no idea that such a termination would take place when he had those visions.

We can see him in our mind's eye sitting on a promontory gazing at the limitless and empty sea. A sail would appear briefly on the horizon, only to disappear again. At least it was some evidence that the real world out there still existed. He must have fashioned a crude sort of calendar to keep track of the days of the week. And the first day of each week he set aside for special religious emphases.

He wrote,

> I was in the Spirit on the Lord's Day, and I heard behind me a loud voice like a trumpet, saying, "Write what you see in a book and send it to the seven churches. . . .' Then I turned to see the voice that was speaking to me, and on turning I saw seven golden lampstands; and in the midst of the lampstands one like a son of man, clothed with a long robe and a golden girdle around his breast; his head and his hair were . . . white as snow; his eyes were like a flame of fire; his feet were like burnished bronze, refined as in a furnace, and his voice was like the sound of many waters; in his hand he held seven stars; from his mouth issued a sharp two-edged sword; and his face was like the sun shining in full strength" (vv. 10-16, RSV).

What an astounding spiritual experience! And I ask, "What if . . . ?" What if he had not been "in the Spirit" on the Lord's Day?

Christianity has always placed great emphasis on the first day of the week. It is our interpretation of the sabbath of the Old Testament. We go back to the creation story in the Book of Genesis. "In the beginning God created the heavens and the earth. . . . And God said, 'Let there be light!' " (Gen. 1:1,3, RSV). This is the Bible's way of announcing the dawn of day one. *Fiat lux!* And creation was!

Then we think of that supreme moment when

> Very early on the first day of the week they [the women] went to the tomb when the sun had risen. And looking up they saw the stone was rolled back. . . . And entering the tomb they saw a young man sitting on the right side, dressed in a white robe. . . . He said, "Do not be amazed;

you seek Jesus of Nazareth who was crucified. *He has risen!*" (Mark 16:2,4-6, RSV, author's italics).

That was the greatest news the world has ever received. It has become the fulcrum of history, the division point in our religious development.

Again, seven weeks later, at the season of Pentecost, also on the first day of the week, the Holy Spirit descended in all His power and glory upon the disciples. That was the day the church of Jesus Christ was born. Is it any wonder that the first day of the week has become the Lord's Day for Christians?

After three centuries, when Constantine ruled the Roman Empire and had become a Christian, he decreed the first Sunday law. The year was AD 321, which historians consider the date when Christianity stepped out of the shadows and became the official religion of the empire. Prior to that Christianity had been either tolerated or subjected to persecution, but from now on it was to grow in grace and influence across the face of the earth.

How, then, are we to observe the Lord's Day, and to share the spirit of the Fourth Commandment as professing Christians? I would offer the following suggestions, and at the same time recognize that each individual must satisfy his own conscience as to the details.

*First*, change the tempo of your life. Change everything possible, including your daily routine. Stay away from your work, with a few necessary exceptions, of course. (Jesus never told a farmer he should not feed his livestock on the sabbath, or refuse to rescue the "ox in the ditch.") Plan different activities, develop different interests, change the scene.

Herman Wouk, the popular novelist, has written a brief autobiography, titled, *This Is My God*, in which he described his way of keeping the sabbath as a pious Jew.

He said he refuses to do any business on that day, whether that means using the telephone, receiving visitors, or going to an office. On one occasion a publisher needed a brief conference with him before his latest book could be sent to the press. Time was vital, or so the publisher thought, but Wouk refused to discuss the matter until the sabbath was over. When the incident became history, the publisher said to him, "I do not envy you your religion, but I envy you your Sabbath." We admire a man who has such deep religious convictions, and lives by them.

*Second*, give your soul a chance. Notice that the Fourth Commandment says at the outset, "Remember the sabbath day, to *keep it holy*" (Author's italics). We think of it as a day of rest, and it is; but that is a secondary consideration. First and foremost, it is a day when we allow our souls to expand in unbounded praise, when we enlarge our understanding of our faith, and when we draw closer to our God as well as to our fellow Christians.

People often say to me, "I wish I had more time to study the Bible." My answer is quite direct: "Well, here's your chance—once every week!" Take, for example, our Scripture lesson for this sermon. It is composed of selections from the first chapter of the Book of Revelation; and as I have said Sunday after Sunday, "This afternoon why not read the entire chapter, or the entire book?" Today is the day to reach out to new and abiding truth from God's Word.

As an aside I might add this. People often say, "I wish you would teach us more about the Book of Revelation; it's too deep for me; I can't understand it." My reply is, "I am ready and anxious to teach this book, or any other portion of Scripture; for, 'where two or three of us are gathered together,' our Lord will be in the midst of us and I will jump at the opportunity. But don't think the Book of Revelation is too deep for you. It is really one of the simplest and most direct treatises in the Bible. It has just one major message: Victory!"

Of course, there is a great deal of imagery, many figures of speech, and not a few innuendoes. Some of these we can unveil; others are lost to history; but the primary message comes through loud and clear. Here is the triumph of righteousness over unrighteousness, of good over evil, of the victory of Christ's kingdom over the kingdoms of this world. In the vernacular, read the Book of Revelation and find out how the story comes out—the guys in the white hats win over the guys in the black hats!

Give your soul a chance; give your mind an opportunity to expand; and give your body a means of regaining both strength and composure.

My own schedule is obviously different from most members of the congregation. The Lord's Day is the most challenging and exacting of all the days of the week for a preacher, and therefore I must choose another as my "sabbath." When that day arrives I keep it as inviolate as possible. On the other days I go into my study to build sermons, dig more deeply into the Scriptures, take care of a multitude of administrative details, offer the best help I can give to those in distress, write, preach, teach, attend important meetings, and so much more. But on my "sabbath" I keep out of my study; more often than not I keep away from the telephone (or unplug it), and try to turn my mind from the problems of the ministry. But when that day is over, I return to my God-given work with renewed enthusiasm, a broader perspective, and a rejuvenated spirit.

*Third,* make the Lord's Day a family day. We are constantly being pulled apart as a family. Everyone seems to go in a different direction—the kids are off to school, Dad, Mother, or both are off to work, the household needs are demanding, community activities absorb our energies, church functions keep us busy. Doctors don't make house calls; we go to them (or to the hospital). Transportation can whisk us hundreds of miles away in a brief span of time—all of which keeps us breathless—and apart!

But the Lord's Day can bring us together. We begin with the emphasis with which the Fourth Commandment begins—keep it holy! Worship lifts our souls. The closer we come to our Lord, the closer we are together. The day is not encumbered with Dad's briefcase full of office details he must get ready for Monday at the office. We don't need to do the weekly shopping on Sunday when we can be together on a picnic, or in the pool, or visiting loved ones.

I had a close friend who was the head of an outlet chain that reached across the United States and Canada. When he was at the peak of his career as a merchant he had more than six hundred stores in his business empire, and he was on the road for long periods of time. His wife told me he would often be as far away as Chicago, or some other city, as the weekend approached, but on Friday night he would board a train in order to get to his hometown in time to teach his senior-high Sunday School class on Sunday morning. Then, on Monday he would be off again to pick up his itinerary where he had left it. He wanted to be with his family, with his son in that class, and in his church at worship.

I think we held the record in our community for having the teacher who made the longest trip each week to be with his Sunday School class. He was an officer in the air force, stationed at Thule, Greenland, the most remote point on the DEW Line. We had three sessions of Sunday School in those days, one at 9:30, a second at 11:00 in the morning, and a third at 6:30 in the evening. Our friend taught a junior-high class in the evening. His own son was in that class, and he accepted his share of the educational leadership of the church. As he taught, his wife would be waiting in the car ready to take him back to a nearby air force base as soon as he finished. There he would be flown back to the Arctic to resume his important work for his country. But on the Lord's Day he was with his family, sharing a spiritual experience.

Another friend was a butcher in our suburban community. He told me of the wonderful times he and his family had had on the Lord's Day when he was a boy. Those were during the Great Depression when money was scarce, but his father would pile his whole family in their car (in near-junk condition) and off they would go together. It would be a visit to grandparents, or an outing in the nearby countryside, or, once in a while, a glorious trip to the shore. Their pleasures were simple, with a minimum of expense involved, but the family shared a genuine fellowship.

And when my friend grew to have children of his own, he carried on the tradition. His wife taught the little tots in the Sunday School; he took his turn at ushering at the worship services; his boys shared the youth activities in the church; and he himself was one of the best Scout leaders we ever had. The Lord's Day was family day for them; and what a joyous occasion it was! He never went near the butcher shop on that day.

I am not advocating a return to the "blue laws," where the emphasis was on strictures rather than spiritual expansion. But the Lord's Day is our passport to freedom. It is our opportunity to change the tempo of life, and our life-style. We need a change of environment, new interests, a new pace, and new faces to see and with whom to associate. It is a day to give our souls a chance to grow, to worship with our fellow Christians, to be in *the best com-*

*pany* (even if a few seem to be hypocrites!) And it is our day to share the priceless privilege of family fellowship.

A man came to my office one day with a serious problem involving his son. He was brokenhearted over the events that had taken place. We talked together for a long time, looked at the situation from every conceivable angle. I offered as much help and counsel as I could. We prayed together, and the tension began to ease. Then as the conference was drawing to a close he bowed his head and said, "I guess I was too busy making money while the boy was growing up."

Don't let that happen in your family. Remember, the Fourth Commandment teaches us to make the Lord's Day the happiest day of the week, the day when we draw closer together as we draw closer to our living Lord. What a blessing! Don't miss the fun!

# 3
# Something Infinitely Precious

## by Norman Vincent Peale

In my apartment in New York I keep a little time machine. It's an old-fashioned doorbell, the kind with a key that you twirl to make it ring. It came from the front door of my grandparents' home in Lynchburg, Ohio, (population 1,000) where my brother Bob and I spent our summers as children.

A lot of water has flowed under the bridge since then. But whenever I want to go back to that little town, all I have to do is turn the key gently, and the roar of the Manhattan traffic grows dim, and pressures fade away, and I'm eight years old again, and all around me is Lynchburg drowsing in the first decade of this century, just as real as it ever was.

I can see it all so plainly: the three churches (Methodist, Baptist, Carmelite); the white frame houses, each with its broad front porch, big maples overhead, and usually a barn or a stable out back; the little railroad station where the B. & O. came through; the livery stables along the main street.

The people are just as real to me, too. See that somewhat stern-looking gentleman over there with the gold watch chain and the bowler hat? That's my Uncle Herschel—Herschel Henderson—coming home for midday dinner. Uncle Herschel is a bank, an insurance company, a building and loan association—a leading citizen. First man in Lynchburg to own an automobile. He doesn't drive it much, and won't let anyone else drive it; he just likes to own it.

Uncle Herschel's a strict disciplinarian; he's always leading his two sons—my cousins Philip and Howard—out to the woodshed for sessions with a razor strop. Doesn't seem to cause any neuroses, though. I doubt if anyone in Lynchburg ever heard of one.

Uncle Herschel's a rock-ribbed Republican, so rock-ribbed that when William Jennings Bryan came through town on the train and made a speech from the observation car's platform, Uncle Herschel wouldn't even come out of his office to hear him. Probably heard him anyway, though; Bryan's voice carried for about half a mile. I was spellbound.

That quiet-looking fellow over there, that's my Uncle George DeLaney. You wouldn't know it to look at him, but he's the greatest cornet player in Ohio, maybe in the whole country. Saturday nights when they have a concert at the bandstand, everyone turns out to hear Uncle George's amazing trills and silvery runs. Sometimes he goes off with the circus and plays in their band for a few weeks. Then he comes back and shows up at Sunday dinner the same as ever.

There on the edge of town you can see the distillery. That's run by Uncle Otto, who married into the family. Nobody's very comfortable about Uncle Otto's occupation. He tries his best to disassociate himself from the Demon Rum. "I make it," he says; "the fools drink it!"

See that corner over there? That's where my father first saw my mother. He was standing in Peale Brothers' Store (general merchandise) and he looked out and saw a new girl in town passing by. He gave a long, low whistle and asked, "Who's that?" "Anna DeLaney." somebody told him. "I'm going to marry that girl," my father said. And he did.

Peale Brothers' Store was not exactly a roaring success, and one reason was the checker games that used to go on in the little back room, presided over by my Uncle Wilson —we called him Uncle Wilse. "Shush!" he'd whisper if an exasperated customer was heard banging on the counter in the unattended store. "Maybe if we keep quiet she'll go away." The result was that finally there were no customers, but Uncle Wilse's reputation as a checker player spread far and wide.

I have one vivid and melancholy memory of another uncle, William Peale. It was a Sunday, and everyone was coming to dinner at my grandparents' house. In those days there was a dreadful custom of calling on children to perform before the assembled guests—play a piece on the piano, or recite something. I had a premonition and hid in the woodshed. But Uncle Will found me and dragged me to the parlor where, with shaking knees and quavering voice, I stumbled through that lachrymose epic, "The boy stood on the burning deck . . ."

Those Sunday dinners were the high point of Sunday, though, just as Sunday was the high point of the week. Oh, summer weekdays were fine for small boys. You could go swimming in the creek, clothes hung on bushes, all girls excluded. You could go down to the station at four o'clock to watch the train come through. If somehow you had acquired a nickel you could go to the picture show at the Bijou on Saturday afternoon. But Sundays had a different tempo, a stately quality. Sundays were where life got its meaning and purpose.

Those Sundays really began on Saturday night. First there were chores to be done: Sunday school lessons studied, coal-oil lamps trimmed and cleaned, food prepared in advance for dinner the next day—Grandma wouldn't

cook on Sunday. Baths for grubby, small boys in the kitch-
en or the wash shed, water from the pump heated on the
wood stove and poured into two tin tubs, one soapy, one
for rinsing. Then upstairs to the big, old double bed where
Grandma, half-moon glasses sliding down her nose, would
read us a story from *Youth's Companion* or *The Christian
Advocate*. She'd hear our prayers and pray over us herself.
Then without fail she'd peer cautiously under the bed.
Once I asked Grandma what she'd do if she found a bur-
gler hiding there. She said serenely that the Lord would
tell her what to do. I was sure He would.

Then she'd kiss us good-night and go away down the
hall, the yellow light of the lamp receding as she went
downstairs until we were in total darkness—and glad of
each other's company.

Next morning when the sun rose it looked down on a
town where virtually every activity that was not church-
related had stopped. The basic idea of Sunday was simple,
really: It was time to turn away from mundane or commercial things and give yourself to your church, your
family, your relatives, and your neighbors. Casual diver-
sions were put aside. No movies on Sunday; the theater
was closed. No organized sports; we kids might sneak in
a game of tag, but we weren't supposed to play ball. Everyone went to Sunday School. And this was followed by
church, also for all ages.

The church was always packed. In those days many
churches had Scripture passages cut into the beams or
painted on the walls: "Remember now thy Creator"
. . . "Peace be within thy walls" . . . "Come unto Me"
. . . "Holiness unto the Lord." Our church also had an
all-seeing eye painted on the wall behind the pulpit. It
was not a stern or baleful eye, but it did effectively remind
small boys that no unworthy activity could escape God's
gaze.

Families sat together with the father at one end of the pew, children next, and mother at the other end. Little boys sat scrubbed in their Sunday suits and squeaky shoes; little girls in hair ribbons and white dresses. All the ladies wore gloves. I can still remember the kid-glove smell that emanated from Grandma's end of the pew where she sat erect and attentive in her dark dress with a cameo pinned to her bosom.

And the grand old hymns, which everyone knew by heart. And the sermons, which could be long. Sometimes an impatient listener might surreptitiously consult a gold watch with a protective case. If he snapped the case shut, the sound might echo all over the church and the minister, glaring down furiously, would remind his audience that this was *his* pulpit and *his* sermon and he would make it as long or as short as he pleased.

After church, everyone went home for Sunday dinner. Uncles and aunts came two by two (followed by cousins), like the animals in the ark, each aunt bearing a dish that was her contribution to the meal. All the women put on aprons and went into the kitchen. The men smoked and talked. Small boys fought for the honor of cranking the ice-cream freezer, the ice chipped from a great burlap-wrapped cake in the cellar and sprinkled with rock salt. The reward was the privilege of licking the dasher when it was removed from the churn.

The meal at the big extended dining-room table began with Bible reading and a prayer. And what a meal! Platters heaped with crisp fried chicken and roasted meat. Mounds of snowy mashed potatoes streaming with golden butter. Gravy boats where you could see little yellow flecks of hard-boiled eggs making the rich sauce even richer. Hot biscuits and vegetables of every kind. Iced tea or lemonade to drink. The only thing I don't remember was salad. Nobody ever mentioned diets or calories, ei-

ther. The food was God's gift, a sign of His goodness.
People were supposed to eat it. They ate it.

After dinner came the part of Sunday I liked best. The
men carried the rockers from the porch out onto the lawn
and arranged them in a circle under the great maple
trees. We youngsters could sit on the grass inside the
circle, if we liked, and listen while they talked. And marvelous talk it was! They discussed the sermon of the morning, thoughtfully, not critically. And the fortunes of the
Cincinnati Reds. And crops. And sometimes politics—but
not too much after a heavy meal. And finally, when all the
standard topics were dealt with, they would begin to tell
stories.

Uncle Herschel might tell of his first trip down the Ohio
on a flatboat. Uncle George would spin tales of circus life.
The Civil War always came up because some of these men
had actually been in it. "Come on, Sam," someone would
say to Grandpa. "Tell us how your company stopped that
Rebel charge at Chickamauga." And Grandpa would tell
them. In those Civil War stories there was never any
bitterness, never any disparagement of the vanquished
foe. They were considered brave men, honorable adversaries who happened to be fighting for the wrong cause,
that was all.

Through all the talk came a quiet pride in the nation
and complete confidence in its future. We had won the
Spanish-American War, hadn't we? We were building the
Panama Canal, weren't we? The French had failed at it,
but we wouldn't, you could count on that. Yes, there were
still problems to be overcome and challenges to be met,
but Christianity was on the march, man with all his faults
was still a perfectable creature, the country was strong,
the future was bright.

Finally, when everyone was talked out, Grandpa might
take us for a ride in his surrey. Out we'd go along Grady

Road, the tasseled whip (never used) swaying in its socket on the dashboard, out past the distillery, past the cemetery, along the dusty road so narrow that if you met another buggy or wagon you had to pull off to the side. Five miles per hour, at the most ten, through the long, lazy Sunday afternoon. No hurry, no strain, no stress. The horse knew the way; if he stopped to snatch a mouthful of sweet grass, nobody cared. Then home at last to a supper of cold meat and cold chicken, and afterward a few hymns perhaps with Aunt Mae playing the wheezy old melodeon. Or maybe just sitting in the porch swing watching the stars come out, and the fireflies beginning to sparkle in the lilac bushes, and the oil lamps being lit in the houses along the quiet street.

Was it all as idyllic as I'm making it sound? No, not all of it. In those days children still died of diphtheria or were crippled by polio. Alcoholism was widespread, despite the thunders from the pulpit, and there was no Alcoholics Anonymous to help. Privies were cold and uncomfortable; in most houses indoor plumbing was still a dream. No electricity meant no appliances; housewives worked long, hard hours cooking and cleaning and washing.

But the basics of life were rock-solid. Marriage was forever; divorce was almost unheard of. Honesty in business was taken for granted. A man was supposed to work hard, keep his word, and pay his debts; if he didn't he was regarded not as evil so much as weak. Evidently, crime didn't pay; there was little of it. Drugs were just a form of medicine. Pornography was beneath contempt. Politics were concerned mainly with state and local issues; Washington seemed dim and far away. People didn't travel much. Why should they, when the rich soil needed tending and children needed raising, and right at home was the tight-woven supportive network of family and neighbors, and the church to point to the eternal verities, and the flag bright against the sky?

They were not spectacular people, perhaps, but I wonder sometimes if we haven't shortchanged them a bit in our history books. When we're asked who built America we're conditioned to think of Pilgrims and frontiersmen and covered wagons and pioneers. And they did indeed conquer the wilderness. But these quiet, solid people two or three generations ahead of us gave us values. They gave us pride and patriotism, and honor and uprightness. They gave us neighborliness, and loyalty to God, and love of family. They gave us morality, and in so doing they gave us strength. And when you look back at them you can't help wondering whether modern America hasn't lost something—something infinitely precious—and doesn't know it.

In my grandmother's backyard, I remember, was a tree loaded with marvelous fruit—damson plums I believe they were called. Every summer we waited impatiently for the plums to ripen, and when they did no fruit ever tasted sweeter. Through the years I've searched in many places for such plums. But I've never found one, and I never will, because the sweetness was not just in the plums. It was the taste of childhood. And when that goes, it goes forever.

But the memories remain, and when I twirl my doorbell key they all come flooding back. I can see the farms where a bell summoned the workers from the fields for midday dinner, and the washbasins on the back porch, and the combs hanging from chains, and the mirrors that always seemed to be crooked. I can hear the owner of the land saying grace—not a hurried blessing but a real prayer—the sunburned faces bowed, the work-roughened hands folded.

I remember the country churches where the great

green ocean of corn seemed to lap at the threshold, and the wagons and buggies hitched under the trees where the horses snorted and stamped. I can see my father preaching in his swallowtail coat, fishing a handkerchief from a pocket in the tails to mop his perspiring forehead, telling the people what Jesus had done for him and what Jesus would do for them if they would just accept Him in their hearts. I can see my mother listening, full of pride, and through the open windows I can hear the sleepy whistle of quail and the sigh of the wind in the trees.

. . .

Sunday. American Sunday. When I was a small boy. Long, long ago.*

# 4
# The Rise of the American Sabbath Union

by Donald S. Stewart

We shall briefly examine some of the background material which led to the founding of the American Sabbath Union and the founding convention itself during mid-December of 1888. From this all-too-brief sketch, I shall attempt to share my own reflections on nearly a century of service which has been, and is still being, so well rendered by The Lord's Day Alliance. This background material is most fascinating and really deserves more than the brief treatment which is possible in this chapter. This is the story of men and women of vision and faith who struggled to translate their dreams into reality. From their successes and failures there is much for us to learn today.

One of the first expressions by American Christians about the keeping of the sabbath occurred in 1810 when Congress passed "a law that post offices should be open and mail carried every day of the week—including Sunday."[1] The passage of this bill touched off a steady flow of protests and resolutions to Congress which culminated in the Sunday Mail Bills of 1829-1830. After fierce debate, these bills were defeated in Congress. But Christians of all denominations continued to hammer away at the problem. Methodists, for example, were sharply divided on the issue of slavery in 1844. They spoke, however, with one voice on the concern for the sabbath in this resolution:

Resolved, That it be the duty of all our preachers to enforce frequently from the pulpit the divine obligation which all are under to keep the Sabbath Day holy; being fully convinced that, were this precept blotted from the decalogue, and men left without the restraints which it imposes, religion (and of course morality) would cease to exert their saving and hallowed influences.[2]

This statement, which is typical of many denominational statements of that day, represents the idea that for American Christians the vision of God for the new world could be fulfilled by working together for true religion and opposing alien influences that were not in harmony with their goals. The great crucible of the Civil War served to sharpen these hopes and to focus with renewed vigor on the goal of a Christian sabbath. And in this light we can see the two primary causes for the founding of the American Sabbath Union.

The first cause was the Civil War (1861-1865) itself. Many religious bodies, North and South alike, decried the abandonment of the sabbath during the harsh years of the conflict. We read, for example, in the "Minutes of the General Assembly of the Presbyterian Church in the Confederate States for 1862" that "the desecration of the holy Sabbath is another crying sin of our land, which we fear abounds in our army."[3] Or, in the North, the "Minutes of the National Council of Congregational Churches of the United States" tell us that:

Owing to the demoralization consequent on the late civil war, and the laxity of all moral restraints growing inevitably from such social disturbances; owing to the introduction and acceptance of transatlantic theories and practices; owing to the mixed character of our great population, representing too many divergent types of thought, to say nothing of the deep-seated, subtle, and pervasive *opposition* of our fallen nature to such claims as emphasize the authority and sovereign ownership of God, Sabbath desecration has assumed alarming proportions, and summons the churches of Christ to a new and vigorous campaign for its repression.[3]

The second cause, which was hinted at in the statement by the Congregational churches, is more subtle and reveals some ugly nativist American attitudes against the large influx of immigrants from continental Europe. These were harsh and, by our standards of today, unchristian statements against the continental sabbath and various groups of immigrants made primarily by the "religious" Americans. In Boston, the residual legacy of the Know-Nothing party of the 1820s to 1860s, which was sworn to keeping Irish Catholics out of power, was still strong. During the years after the Civil War the American Protective Association rallied some New England Protestants to their cause with the claim that the Roman Catholic Church was against keeping Sunday as the Lord's Day and that the Catholic school system was anti-American. This controversy died down only as Catholics gained political power in Boston in the persons of Patrick A. Collins and "Honey Fitz" Fitzgerald and as the Massachusetts Legislature passed the "Wardwell Bill" of 1888. This bill made education by freedom of choice the law, so that parents could either send their children to a public or approved private school.

Paradoxically, one of the best statements on sabbath observance was made by the "immigrant," Swiss-born, German-educated Philip Schaff, the well-known theologian and church historian of the later nineteenth century. He maintained that:

> Our separation of church and state rests on mutual respect and friendship, and is by means a separation of the nation from Christianity. The religious Sabbath cannot and ought

not to be enforced by law; for all worship and true religion must be free and voluntary homage of the heart. But the civil Sabbath can and ought to be maintained and protected by legislation; and a Christian community has a natural right to look to their government for the protection of their Sabbath as well as for the protection of their persons and property.[4]

So the movement for a Sabbath Union of concerned Christians and denominations grew rapidly during the postwar years. Various church denominations issued calls for sabbath observance by their members and for the nation as a whole. These pronouncements were both a summons to battle by Christians and the affirmation that the American sabbath was a unique virtue which must be preserved at all costs.

The Congregational Church National Council's pronouncement of 1871 serves as a vivid example of what most American religious bodies were saying and thinking.

Amidst the multiplied activities and enlarging enterprises which engross the mind and conserve the strength of our citizens, the rest of the Sabbath is indispensible to the continuance of health, virtue and Christian principle in this nation.[5]

It is of interest to note that while a variety of denominations pressed for action on both religious and political fronts, the major political parties were opposed to any congressional legislation. The Republican Party platform of 1872 articulated this viewpoint in these words:

The Republican Party proposes to respect the rights reserved by the people to themselves as carefully as the powers delegated by them to the State and Federal Government. It disapproves of the resort to unconstitutional laws for the purpose of removing evils by interfereing with the rights not surrendered by the people. We favor the discountenacing of all Sunday Laws and this upon the ground of conserving the rights of the people such as the right to look upon the day on which Christians have their prayer meeting as any other day.[6]

U.S. Grant was reelected upon this platform and supported it as is evidenced by his willingness to accept the platform without any changes in this particular plank. In May of 1888 the General Conference of the Methodist Episcopal Church passed a strong resolution calling for the immediate establishment of a national and ecumenical sabbath committee. Almost simultaneously this initiative was followed most energetically by Presbyterians—North and South—Baptist, and Congregational churches. A committee was formed from various denominational representatives and a meeting was set to establish the Sabbath Union. The meeting was held at historic Foundry Methodist Episcopal Church in Washington, D. C. from December 11 to 13, 1888. At the same time as the committee announced its plans, a National Sabbath Bill was introduced in both houses of Congress. This bill, with substantial bipartisan support, was designed to augment and support existing state sabbath laws. In the Senate, Bill number 2983 was introduced by Senator H. W. Blair and stated that

no person or corporation shall perform any secular labor, work or business; nor shall any person engage in any play, game, amusement or recreation on the first day of the week commonly known as the Lord's Day.[7]

The convention in December would not only form the American Sabbath Union, but call attention to the bill and provide the members of the denominations represented to engage in the time-honored practice of lobbying the congress on behalf of the bill.

As the time for the convention drew near, the city of Washington became increasingly aware that this would not be an ordinary convention, but one of great significance! For example, petitions with many thousands of signatures favoring the National Sabbath Bill began to arrive from all over the nation. Newspapers carried large advertisements offering all convention-goers one-third-reduced fare for round-trip rail tickets on many of the leading railroads. Other ads told of many places in Washington where the visitors could obtain room and board for the convention. Three meals a day were offered at a special rate of $1.25 a day!

When the convention began on December 11, 1888, it was front-page news in both *The Washington Post* and *The Washington Evening Star*. The lead article in the *Post* began with these words:

> The First National Sabbath Convention will meet tonight at Foundry Church with Col. Elliott F. Shepherd of the *New York Mail and Express* presiding. The church will be decorated in a novel manner. About the gallery will be suspended shields of the Union States represented in the convention from which will be festooned long lists of petitions for the passage of the pending Sabbath Observance Bill posted on red cotton cloth, five thousand yards of cloth with the signatures of 13 million people.[8]

The census for 1890 shows a population of 62,947,714 for the nation. The 13 million signatures represented, therefore, about 18 percent of the population of the nation in 1888. The *Christian Advocate for New York* noted that a "large proportion of the signers of this petition are members of labor organizations who feel the tyrany of Sabbath toil."[9] It is of interest to note that at the time of its founding and during its earliest years, the American Sabbath Union had a strong identification with the fledging labor movement in this country. As the twenty-fifth

anniversary report of The Lord's Day Alliance, General
Secretary, Reverend H. L. Bowlby stated:

> The Alliance has been a great benefactor to the Sons of
> Labor. Many victories have been won for men seeking rest
> from toil on the Lord's Day. If you rob the working man
> of that rest, you rob him of light and air and thus slay
> him.[10]

A review of records will also show that the Knights of
Labor and other unions gave heavy financial support to
the work of The Lord's Day Alliance in its early years.

Briefly, the convention consisted of three days of
speeches, lectures, and sermons at Foundry Church and
intense lobbying by the delegates on Capitol Hill. A group
of fifty representatives went, on the afternoon of December
14, 1888 to see lame-duck President Grover Cleveland. The president graciously received the group but
made no promises about signing the bill. The typical tone
and appeal of the convention messages come through
most clearly in these words of J. M. Buckley of New York.
He said that this important national meeting

> is one of the most significant and timely movements of this
> generation. It is high time that all friends of the Sabbath
> rally to its defense. The wise men who laid the foundations
> of this nation understood the value of this day of rest and
> made provision for its observance, protection and per-
> petuity.[11]

There were a number of fascinating aspects about the
convention. One which really impressed me was the
strong sense of ecumenical support and participation
among Christians of various denominations for this alliance. One of the signers of the petition was James Cardinal Gibbons of the Catholic Church in Baltimore. Gibbons
was known throughout his ministry for a strong concern
for the preservation of the sabbath and for the laboring

person. He saw the Sabbath Union as a natural extension of that pastoral concern. He wrote this letter to the National Sabbath Committee:

> I am most happy to add my name to those of the millions of others who are laudably contending against the violation of the Christian Sabbath by unnecessary labor, and who are endeavoring to promote decent and proper observance by legitimate legislation. The due observance of the Lord's Day contributes immeasurably to the restriction of vice and immorality, and to the promotion of peace, religion and social order, and cannot fail to draw upon the nation the blessing and protection of overruling providence.[12]

Gibbons was nominated for the executive committee of the Sabbath Union but declined in favor of a Father DeColgan who was vicar-general in Baltimore. This early ecumenism was noted in *The Washington Evening Star* in its coverage of the convention for December 12, 1888. It said: "Christian Charity and Harmony in the Convention —Catholics and Quakers invited to join—A Catholic made member of first Executive Committee."[13]

So much for the founding of The American Sabbath Union in December, 1888. The bill which those founding members sought was killed in committee—lost in the election and transition shuffle of 1888 which saw Benjamin Harrison elected President of the nation. The record of its founding and early years has many tales of courageous individuals and corporate Christian action. These people struggled earnestly with the problem—which still confronts us today—of how to make our faith a force in the common life of this great nation. I believe one way we can do this is by our personal influence.

Two years ago I spent a period of time in Israel in study and travel in that ancient and war-torn land. While there,

I noted something fascinating about the sabbath. On Friday afternoon in Israel, the Jewish shops close and the people in distinctive sabbath dress head toward their places of worship. The Jewish shops and stores stay closed until sundown Saturday evening. The Moslem people of Israel close their shops and stores on Thursday afternoon and they remain closed through the main time of prayer at the mosque on Friday noon at which all of the faithful are expected to be present. On Sunday, the Christian community closes its shops and stores and is engaged in worship and rest that is familiar to each of us. The beautiful thing about all of this is that it works and each tradition uses its sabbath to worship and praise God.

I was in the shop of an Arab Christian in Jerusalem one Friday afternoon looking at his rich collection of antiquities. This man, named Mr. Kando, was one of the first to see the Dead Sea Scrolls and to realize their value for the world. While there, a tourist bus of Americans descended on his shop and the people began to look and make the decision of whether to buy an item. One woman simply could not decide on an item and said to Mr. Kando, "I can't make up my mind, but I'll come back on Sunday and make my choice." Mr. Kando said simply: "Madam, we are all Christians here, our store is closed on Sunday." The woman went off muttering about these strange foreigners and I went away rejoicing.

Another way we demonstrate our concern for the sabbath is by our action in support of the Lord's Day League here in New England. The words of Dr. David G. Wylie, spoken at the twenty-fifth anniversary meeting of The Lord's Day Alliance in 1913, speak eloquently of our need to continue the ninety-two-year tradition of service. He said:

We are not poorer but richer, because we have, through

the ages, rested from our labor one day in seven. That day is not lost while industry is suspended, while the plow lies in the furrow, while the exchange is silent, while no smoke ascends from the factory, but a process is going on. Man, the maker of machines is repairing and winding up, so that he returns to his labors with clearer intellect, with livelier spirits, with renewed vigor. The day of rest gives pause, time to consider the aims of life and so develops us morally and spiritually.[14]

God has given to all people the unique opportunity to engage in worship and in rest; to celebrate God's presence in our lives and in the lives of others, and to work for the betterment of all mankind in our world. And all of this is based on our freely honoring that one day of worship. Come, let us say that our faith is in the Lord and in the Lord do we trust, and worship, and serve all the days of our lives and truly we shall dwell in the house of the Lord forever.

### Notes

1. Robert L. Handy, *A Christian America*, "Protestant Hopes and Historical Realities" (New York, Oxford University Press, n.d.), p. 48.

2. Handy, p. 49.

3. Minutes of the General Assembly of the Presbyterian Church in the Confederate States of America, 1862, p. 37. Long after the war Benjamin W. Jones, R. L. Dabney, and James H. Thornwell believed that God withdrew from the South because of the general and shameful violation of the sabbath.

3. Handy, p. 85.

4. Handy, p. 86.

5. Handy, p. 84.

6. *American State Papers Bearing On Sunday Legislation*, compiled and edited by William A. Blakely (New York: Da Capo Press, reprint of original 1911 edition, 1970) p. 169.

7. American State Papers, pp. 360-361.

8. *The Washington Post*, December 11, 1888, p. 1.

9. *The Christian Advocate for New York*, December 1888, p. 833.

10. *Annual Report of The Lord's Day Alliance,* Twenty-fifth Anniversary, 1913, p. 10.

11. *Christian Advocate,* p. 833.

12. American State Papers, p. 228.

13. *The Washington Evening Star,* December 12, 1888, p. 1.

14. *Annual Report, The Lord's Day Alliance,* p. 14.

(Note: For a good treatment of religious bigotry in Boston, see Gustavus Myers, *History of Bigotry in the United States* (New York Random House, 1943), pp. 219-247.)

# 5
# The Sabbath Was Made for Mankind

*Mark 2:27*

by Frederick Brown Harris

*(Editor's Note: After an interesting introduction in which he called attention to the meaning and purpose of the day, and the perplexing problems and conflicting attitudes that have arisen with the sabbath of today and that of a hundred years ago, Dr. Harris went directly into his theme—that the law of the sabbath is written in human hearts and guards their highest interests of body, mind, and spirit. The sermon then moves on as follows:)*

I want rather to think with you of the use of that which we call the Lord's Day which will best keep us within the good graces of the law which is written in our own hearts and in the very constitution of the universe, a law which guards the highest interests of our bodies, our minds, and our immortal spirits. For my contention is that after all there is basically no conflict as to whether this one day in seven is to be thought of as the Lord's Day or as mankind's day, for when it is honestly used as our day it is most truly the Lord's Day. As we follow the Master, whom we acknowledge as the Lord of the sabbath, through the scenes of His earthly ministry and watch what He does with the sabbath, and on the sabbath, in spite of the angry protests of the literalists who kept its letter and lost its spirit, there can be no doubt that He was giving expression to the fundamental governing principle when He said of it, "[It] was made for man" (Mark 2:27). It should be used for people. A study of Christ's attitude to the sabbath day convinces me that Jesus had three tests for sabbath keeping. First, it is a day of restoration. Second, it is a day of inspiration. Third, it is a day of adoration.

## Day of Restoration

Very much is included in that conception of the sabbath as a day of restoration. Through the centuries it has been called a "day of rest." That very term emphasizes the ministry of the sabbath to the body. There can be no question that Christ emphasized that. What emphasis the New Testament puts upon the human body. The body! That harp of a thousand strings which dies if one is gone. In the first Christian centuries little attention seemed to be given to the New Testament emphasis on the physical. Those first-century Christians seemed to think of it as distinctly a Book of the Soul, to be read while they beat their bodies into subjection.

But there is no Book in literature which so dignifies the body. Paganism knows nothing of the New Testament conception of the human body, as it declares: "Know ye not that your [bodies are temples]?" (1 Cor. 6:19). The fallacy of the monastery idea, and that which finally overthrew the system, was that it spurned the body which the Scriptures exalt. It is extraordinary how many folks have sought to be wiser than the Bible and have tried to be a little more spiritual than Christ. It is difficult for many people in our modern churches even yet to see that in its right sphere a gymnasium may be as much a means of grace as a prayer meeting. It was the gospel of Jesus which lifted the body from the mire of paganism and crowned it with honor and glory.

Once more we approach the holy season when we celebrate the wondrous fact that the Word itself became flesh. Through human lips the voice of God spoke. Through human eyes the pity of God looked. With hands like ours He threw open the gates of a new life. The miracles of the New Testament are revelations rather than arguments. They teach us that the body is part of the life which Christ redeems. He did not indulge in mere rhapsodies about the soul when about Him eyes were sightless, feet were maimed, ears were stopped, and tongues were sealed. He was quick, too, to see the telltale marks of bodily fatigue. "Come ye yourselves apart . . . and rest a while" (Mark 6:31). It was Christ's insistence on a holiday.

### The Body Needs Guarding

We have a beautiful hymn, "Jesus, Lover of My Soul." We ought to have another that says, "Jesus, Lover of My Body." We have allowed a system not scientific, and not always Christian, to take a vital part of the teaching of Jesus which we have discarded about the healing of the body. Thank God, the Christian church is showing signs in these latter days of believing and practicing Paul's word to the Ephesians, "He is the Savior of the body." The new gospel of health which is being preached from so many pulpits today, pulpits outside churches, calling attention to the sins against the human body is a part of *our* gospel.

To say over an early grave, in many cases, "Whereas God in His wise providence has taken out of the world the soul of the departed," is a travesty, when the truth is often that rather people in their absolute, willful disregard for the laws of the human body have committed suicide. It is a great and solemn thought that the sabbath was given to minister to the needs of the human body.

A former generation were often breaking the sabbath when they thought they were keeping it. They mistook sanctimoniousness for sanctity, and emptied the sabbath of all sunshine, gladness, and the holiness of beauty. They broke it by putting a taboo on the open air and joyous associations. They broke it by clearing the landscape of all but what they were pleased to call the sacred. They thought by the repression of the body they were clearing the way for the expression of soul, and so Sunday was devitalized and dehumanized.

Henry Ward Beecher once said that he felt on Sunday as though he were a pincushion and that every Sunday duty was like a pin sticking into him. The old-fashioned Sunday was like the old-fashioned parlor, too stuffy, gloomy, and dark. Too often it was forgotten what a wise physician said to his pastor, "The Sabbath law is written on the human body."

### More of God's Son-Day than Golf's Sunday

Now rest in the sense of restoration does not mean necessarily hours of lazy indoor loafing. It means that, so far as its effect on the body is concerned, it will send one back to one's weekly work on Monday with nerves soothed, with the fever and the fret allayed, and with cells refreshed and restored, ready to take up the round of daily duties and obligations with new inspiration, with courage, hope, and patience.

"All right," said an eminent man of whom a prominent New York preacher tells us, "I'll spend the day on the golf links or the trout stream in the interest of my body." "Oh, yes," said this businessman, when questioned, he still believed in religion and required his children to attend church, but for himself he could find wiser uses for the day than to spend it within the cloister. He wanted the sunshine of the golf course rather than the dim religion light of the sanctuary. This particular man had so bowed down at the altar of mammon and lifted up his soul unto vanity that he did not hesitate to assert that it would be merely a question of time when by a judicious use of golf clubs and fishing poles he would be able to commercially outdistance any competitor who used up his energy on Sunday teaching in the church school or attending public worship.

I could take you on any weekday straight to the doors of men in Washington—bankers, businessmen, and teachers—who would not live in any city where there were not churches and where public worship was not conducted, who tell the preacher, "If I am to keep myself fit physically, I must have more out-of-door life, more oxygen, more exercise. Sunday is the only day I can get it. I have nothing against the church—I am for it. I am willing to contribute. I have holy memories of my churchgoing parents, but life today is a drive with numerous tensions under the tremendous pressure to make good that our fathers never knew. I must take Sunday for my body."

### Safety in the Sabbath. Example: A Gentleman

Now I am not here to arbitrarily tell anybody how they can make Sunday what I believe the Lord meant it to be, a day of ministry to the body. That is for every person a matter of conscience. I think a safe rule for recreation on Sunday would be always the application of John Wesley's rule with regard to amusements on all seven days of the week, namely, not to do anything that could not be done in the name of the Lord Jesus.

What a lovely picture it is, full of light and love, relaxation and restoration, as we see Jesus on the sabbath, walking with His disciples, enjoying to the full the glories of the out-of-doors, reveling in all the delight of growing things. The Bible says that his disciples began, as they went, to pluck the ears of corn and to eat. Not a blue Sunday with Jesus. It was a white day: gladness, sunshine, and social intercourse were not cut off. The Pharisees objected to all this. They challenged the claims of the body on the Lord's Day. But Jesus said, "The sabbath was made for man" (Matt. 2:27). Man with a body.

To the person who takes this as an excuse and a justification for handling an automobile wheel or golf sticks on Sunday morning, instead of hymnal and Bible, I want to say just three things. The first is not the word of a preacher, but of a business expert, Roger W. Babson, who pleaded with the businessmen of America thus:

> For our own sakes, for our nation's sake, let us businessmen get behind the churches and their ministers. The safety of all we have is due to the churches. By all that we hold dear, let us from this very day give more time and thought to the churches for upon these the value of all we own ultimately depends.

The second thing I would like to say is this: Has anyone the right to do anything which, if all followed his example, would do more harm than good? And the third, the best definition of a gentleman which I know. George Bernard Shaw said, "A gentleman is a man who always tries to put in a little more than he takes out."

## Day of Inspiration

We come then to the second test of keeping the sabbath. Is it a day of inspiration? Not only a day of breathing out, but a day of breathing in. Christ used it as the great brooding day for the soul, the day on which the soul itself is to take deep breaths. A person must answer for the things he is doing on the Lord's Day; but what about the things a person is not doing? Think of the great multitude of Americans any Sunday who, bent on recreation, think more of perspiration than they do of inspiration—more about oxygen for their lungs and blood than for the breath of the Eternal on their spirits—more about muscle than they do about soul. The question, of course, is not so much what we are doing with Sunday as it is what we are making Sunday do to us.

A missionary to the Indians, seeking to induce habits of sabbath observance, told them that if they planted their corn on Sunday it would not grow. A spirit of human perversity, which we all understand and share, led them immediately to set out and plant an acre of corn on Sunday. They hoed it and tended it always on Sunday and, because they took special pains with it, when autumn came the yield of that acre was more than any other on the reservation. Then the Indians laughed at the good missionary and refused to go to church.

There is a penalty for planting and hoeing corn on Sunday, but it does not show in the corn; it shows in the person. The corn may grow to full size but the people will not grow to full size if they neglect to cultivate human values, soul values, for which the sabbath was given. The result will show in itself in the shriveled souls of those who have no place in the week for the cultivation of reverence, aspiration, and a sense of fellowship with the Unseen.

**Professor Peabody's Warning**

Professor Peabody of Harvard sounded a note of needed warning in these words:

> The real peril of the age is the possibility that among the engrossing interests of modern life there shall be no outlook at all, no open window of the mind, no holy city of the soul—the shutters of life closed, the little things crowding out the great ones, and the soul all unaware of the sunshine and landscape which lie at its very door.

That is the materialism from which any life might pray to be set free—the practical materialism which curses American life—the shut-in, self-absorbed, unspiritualized, shallow life, the life without ideals, the windows toward Jerusalem closed and barred, and the person within too busy to have time to look out on any distant tower of a sanctifying thought.

A gentleman was inspecting a house in Newcastle with a view to renting it, and the landlord took him to an upper window and said, "You can see Durham Cathedral from this window on Sunday."

"Why on Sunday above any other day?" inquired the man.

"Because on that day there is no smoke from these tall chimneys," was the answer.

Every man and woman needs one day in seven where the air will be swept clean of the smoke of commercialism and where the cathedral towers of vision will be the symbol of a day which is itself a sanctuary dedicated to keeping the things of the spirit alive.

Yes, the sabbath was made for mankind—mankind who has a body—mankind who is a soul. It was made for the restoration of the body—for the inspiration of the soul. As we follow once more the Lord of the sabbath, we find that by precept and example He taught that it was made for adoration, for the worship of the Infinite.

### Sabbath and Sanctuary Joined in Wedlock

One of the earliest glimpses of Jesus show Him in the Temple on the sabbath. In His busy manhood we find Him in the synagogue on the sabbath day, as His custom was. No one saw the shams and the shallowness of the churchianity and the pious pretenses of many who were pillars in the church more than Christ, and none rebuked them more scathingly than He, and yet to the end of His ministry He practiced the presence of God in the sanctuary.

"There are few men," said the president of one of our leading educational institutions, "whose spiritual sense will not be quickened, whose aspirations will not be elevated, whose religious ideals will not be ennobled by the fellowship with his brethren which the Christian Church offers."

One of the finest touches I know of in literature with regard to the influence of a church service on the Lord's day, is found in Henry Ward Beecher's story *Norwood.* It is the description of the close of a Sunday morning service in a village church. The village horse jockey and the doctor have just driven up and are waiting for the congregation to come out. While the jockey is pointing out to the doctor the comparative merits of the neighbors' teams standing in the horse shed, the congregation begins to sing the closing hymn.

"There, Doctor, there's the last hymn," the jockey says. It rises upon the air, softened by distance and the enclosure of the building, rises and falls in regular movements. Even Hiram, the jockey's tongue ceases. Again the hymn rises, and this time fuller and louder, as if the whole congregation has caught the spirit. Men, women, and little children's voices are in it. Then the jockey says, without any of his usual pertness, "Doctor, there's somethin' in folks' singin' when you are outside the church, that makes you feel as though you ought to be inside."

And before those of us who are inside the church turn, after the closing hymn to go out, thanking the Lord of the sabbath for this day which was made for man, for His restoration, for inspiration, and for adoration, I shall repeat the last lines of Edwin Ford Piper's vivid poem entitled, "The Church."

A little church: the settlers come for miles.
Some few, unhearing, sit in selfish dreams;
For life is vilely mingled, sweetly mixed,
Scanty or bounteous in vital force;

But here the most are really worshippers,
Seeking in fellowship a sympathy
With God. Their simple faces plainly show
What feelings stir the heart, for hard looks melt,
And thin, worn wretchedness in garb grotesque
Is eased of ugliness while it feeds
On love and hope. This meager hour may lift
Some groveling face to see the blessed sky;
Master a soul, and yield it back to life
Tempered against the evil day to be.
A little thing, this church? Remove its roots,
Ossa upon Pelion would not fill the pit.

—*Lord's Day Leader**

*Used by permission of the Lord's Day League of New England

# 6
# The Lord's Day

by J. McDowell Richards

I need not say to you that today we are in danger of losing our heritage. Our generation knows little about the observance of a "Lord's Day." We don't even talk much about it. How much preaching about the Lord's Day have you heard recently? And how much teaching is being done about—certainly very little in churches with which I am acquainted. Why is it that we have so little to say about a subject which, I believe, is one of crucial importance to the life of the Christian enterprise?

Well, there are various reasons, I suppose, why we don't preach more about it. For one thing, people don't want to hear about it! They resist it. The conscience of some Christians is sensitive on the subject—but for many it is not. These people are often not aware of the fact that there is a question about how to use Sunday. But those who are aware of the problem are doing so little about it that they don't want to be reminded!

A minister in Atlanta told me recently that one of the members of his church, in a desire to show friendship for his pastor, had offered him tickets to the Atlanta Falcons football games, which of course are played almost uniformly on Sunday afternoon. The minister thanked him very much but said, "Well, I don't go to football games on Sunday." This angered the member very much. The fact that the minister would be such an "old fogey" as to not

use football tickets on Sunday afternoon! Such persons
don't want to hear about it.

Again, perhaps we don't preach about the subject more,
or teach it more, because it baffles all of us. How can one
observe the Lord's Day in our age? It was a comparatively
simple thing to do when this was largely an agricultural
economy: when most of our people lived in small towns
and in leisurely days—not that there has ever been very
consistent observance of the day by people as a whole,
even in Israel. The message of the prophets reminds us of
the fact that the Jewish people did not consistently keep
their sabbath through the years. Again, and again, and
again, they had to be called back to the meaning of the
day. But we live in the day of the automobile, the jet
plane, the radio and television, and all the complexity of
late twentieth-century life. How does one fit the Lord's
Day into the context of these times? It is a difficult question.

And, then again, the Lord's Day has been made the
subject of attack and of belittlement, sometimes, unfortu-
nately, by those who are within the ranks of the Christian
fellowship. I heard a man, for example, when this question
was raised on a university campus say, "Well, we can't be
concerned with that—that's just superstition!" Well,
when it was called a superstition, of course, the rest of us
were supposed to be completely demolished.

I think it was Dr. Halford Luccock, who a number of
years ago spoke of the device of substituting an epithet for
an argument. If you can just use the right epithet, you
don't have to argue.

None of us wants to be guilty of cherishing a superstition. It is like telling a person he's narrow-minded, or
old-fashioned, or dogmatic—and that's supposed to end it.
Satan is very astute in the phrases he suggests.

I think about the term "Blue Laws." In an adjoing county in Georgia in the last several weeks, we have been hearing a great deal about this, because the district attorney decided to enforce the Sunday laws. He closed up a large number of business establishments who decided to sell everything that they sell every day in the week. Well, the term, "Blue Law" historically originated because the sabbath legislation in New England was bound in a blue book, but the term today suggests that what we are trying to enforce is a "blue" kind of outlook and a "blue" kind of world. It suggests the kind of Puritanism that doesn't want anybody to be oneself. "Blue Laws"! Well, who's going to stand up and support "Blue Laws," the imposition of gloom and sadness on other people?

But there are also those within the ranks of Christendom who belittle the sabbath day, or would destroy it. Someone approached a leader of one of our principal American denominations in behalf of The Lord's Day Alliance a year or more ago, and the response was, "Well, I'm not too much interested in promoting the observance of the Lord's Day. What I'm interested in is using every day for the Lord."

Well, who isn't? But the fact is, if we have no particular concern for setting aside one day as a time for special worship and remembrance, we are not likely to use the other six days of the week in the service of God. Anyone who's concerned that all days be used aright, had better be concerned about the Lord's Day.

Again, there are those who point to the example of Christ, and note how our Lord departed from the sabbath legislation of His own day, and His righteous statement that "The sabbath was made for man and not man for the sabbath." Well, obviously, that's true. "The Son of man is also Lord also of the sabbath" (Mark 2:27-28). But the sabbath was made, that is appointed—it was "made": certainly not for human physical pleasure primarily, and cer-

tainly not for personal financial gain, but for mankind's
highest goal, which is spiritual. Those to whom I have
referred say, "The letter killeth, but the spirit giveth life"
(2 Cor. 3:6), and in light of this statement proceed to kill
not only the letter, but also the spirit of sabbath observance.

Again, they say, "Well this is not the seventh day of the
week. The Fourth Commandment is, 'Remember the sabbath Day to keep it holy. For in six days the Lord made
heaven and earth . . . and rested the seventh day' " (Ex.
20:8,11). Well, how can we argue for the observance of
the first day of the week as if it were the seventh? Does
change in the day of the week nullify a spiritual principle?
Of course, this change from the seventh day to the first,
is really one of the most remarkable events in Christian
history—in human history, if you think about it. How did
it come about that people who had observed the sabbath
on the seventh day of the week, one in whose lives this
duty was engraved deeply, came to observe the first day
instead? We see evidence of this happening in the New
Testament, and in the practice of the apostles. We see it
evident in the life of the early church when it was still
predominantly led by Jewish leaders. One can study it for
a long time and not fully explain it. Whatever else is true
about it, we assert, with confidence, that it is one of the
supreme evidences of the reality of the resurrection of
Christ. You can't account for it on any other grounds. On
the first day of the week now, we celebrate Christ's completion of the work of redemption, and the hope that is
ours of eternal rest.

But those are the kinds of things that people urge
against our observance of the Lord's Day. Well, human
experience has shown the importance of the Lord's Day
to real religion. One could multiply statements about it.
Of course, one of the most familiar statements is that

attributed to Voltaire who is alleged to have said, "If you would destroy the Christian religion, you must first destroy the Christian Sabbath." In the French Revolution, when they set out to destroy the Christian religion, that's exactly what they did. They outlawed the Christian sabbath. It was not long until they had to come back to it.

We, however, do not outlaw it; we do not set out to destroy it; we simply allow it to go by default. And, my friends, if there is to be strength in the church in the future, we are going to have to find a way, even in our troubled world and complex civilization, to celebrate the Lord's Day.

The early Christians managed to do it in a pagan world where slavery existed. Many of these early Christians were slaves! I'm sure they weren't permitted to rest from labor on the sabbath day, but they found a way to worship God and to make this day holy.

How shall we observe the Lord's Day in our time? There was a day which was greatly concerned about what one must not do on Sunday. I was reared in such a day, and I remember still the things that we were taught not to do. There were certain things which we should carefully avoid on Sunday. There was educational value in this fact.

What we ought to be concerned about, however, is the positive aspect of sabbath observance. What shall we do on the Lord's Day? Well, it is a time for rest. That's one of the things most manifest in the Fourth Commandment —rest. And it wasn't class legislation, either. It was intended for the servants, and even for the animals.

A time for quietness—that's one thing we are concerned about in encouraging the right kind of civil legislation; not to make anybody worship on Sunday if they don't want to, but to see that a person shall have the opportunity to worship if that is her desire, and the opportunity to rest if conscience tells her to do so.

Rest! We need that in our day. Quietness! A little time to be still and to know that God is.

It is a day for the home. The sabbath was kept and was taught in the home, and the home was preserved by the sabbath. If the home is decaying today, and it is, how largely must we attribute this to the fact that there is no real observance of a Lord's Day? Our sabbath time—what greater opportunity for a family to be together? The tragedy today is that we don't live today at home as families. Here is a time to be together, a time to enjoy fellowship with one another; a time for the strengthening of ties between husband and wife; between parents and children—a time for Christian education. Why is it that we are a religiously illiterate people today? Because, for the most part, religion is not taught in the home. If there is no teaching of it on Sunday, there will not be any other time, one may be sure.

During the time in France when the observance of Sunday was outlawed for a few years—during that time divorce in that country multiplied by twenty thousand—a high proportion in the population of that day. Is there any connection between the decay of the Lord's Day in our time and the near explosion in our divorce rate?

Once again, the Lord's Day is a time that calls us to worship in the congregation; it's a time for us to assemble ourselves in the congregation to praise God and hear the preaching of God's Word. Is it important, do you think? Well, there are those who tell us it is not. It's just as possible to worship God on the golf course, they say, or we must go away to the seashore, or to the mountains. It's so beautiful there it reminds us of God. We can't be shut up in a church on such a day of beauty and joy. You can't expect that of us! "Blue Domers," one prominent minister called these people, but how much worship do you suppose is done by them on the golf course, or by the seashore, or even in the mountains? Beauty in God's world reveals His handiwork, but, so far as I know, has seldom changed a human heart.

I went back this summer to the principality of Monaco in southern France, to Monte Carlo, one of the most beautiful spots in all the world—with granite mountains rising from the blue waters of the Mediterranean, with lawns and flowers and palm trees, and the blue sky above. If beauty would make a person better, surely it should be there. But it is not for nobility of character that Monte Carlo is famous.

My first pastorate was in the mountains of North Georgia, a beautiful place. Sometimes I used to say that anyone who lived there ought to be better for it, but as I reflected about it, I found it wasn't true. Some of the best people lived there, but some of the most degraded and sinful lived there, too. There isn't any power in nature to change a human heart. Only the Word of God, the gospel of Christ can change a human heart, and the Lord's Day is a time when we had better not forsake the assembling of ourselves together in His house, for His worship, for the hearing of His word.

And, of course, the Lord's Day gives a great opportunity to do good. It's a time for deeds of mercy, kindness, and love. It's a time for the right kind of Christian fellowship. It's a time for joy!

The German Jewish poet, Heinrich Heine, had a parable of one who six days of the week was a drudge, but who on the seventh day became a princess.

This is a true parable of religious experience which can be ours as we observe the Lord's Day.

One of the most amazing passages in Scripture is the seventeenth chapter of Jeremiah. In reading the Book of

Jeremiah, one finds that it is almost a continuous denunciation of the sins of Israel. Sometimes Jeremiah rose to great hope and to the message of redemption, but he pointed out again and again the sins of Israel. How awful they were! Lying, theft, adultery, murder, idolatry—almost anything you can name—but in the seventeenth chapter of the book, he promised his people that if they would keep the sabbath day the Lord would restore the throne of Israel and the kingdom would be preserved. How could that be?

Well, certainly the prophet was not saying that if you just keep the sabbath day you can go ahead to lie, steal, commit adultery, and murder; all with impunity; just keep the letter of the law. That's not what he meant. Surely what Jeremiah said is this: You have committed all these sins because you have neglected the day on which character is built, the day on which communion with God is especially established. When you come back to using this sabbath day aright, you won't commit these other sins. That message is the one with which I close.

# 7

# When God Gets Radical

by Ernest A. Bergeson

Why does God permit the world to continue with the terrible injustices and corruption that manifest themselves in human society? Recently we have heard the prophets of doom suggesting the end of the world or at least some catastrophic event like a major earthquake because of a planetary conjunction in the heavens. Nothing happened of any note. God seems to be silent in the face of a world dominated by the evil intentions that erupt in the human heart.

We are reminded that in the Old Testament God did enter into the scene with radical actions that were devastating to sinful human beings, such as the Flood at the time of Noah, the nuclear kind of devastation that wiped Sodom and Gomorrah off the face of the earth, the confounding of the tongues at the construction site of the Tower of Babel, and the bringing down of the walls that killed many as Samson's strength was restored to him by God's judgmental hand. And in the New Testament in the gospel lesson for this day, God through our Lord Jesus Christ acts in the only case on record when Jesus was violent, driving the money changers from the Temple and declaring, "Get out of here! How dare you turn my Father's house into a market!" Matthew quoted Jesus in even stronger and more radical terms: "It is written, 'My house shall be called a house of prayer'; but you make it a den of robbers' " (21:13, RSV). Mark in the same radical tone had Him putting it in question form: "Is it not written, 'My house shall be called a house of prayer for all the nations'? But you have made it a den of robbers" (11:17, RSV). Matthew carried the words of Jesus even farther as he described His preaching in the Temple and how on leaving the Temple He talks with His disciples. They begin pointing out what a great complex of buildings the Temple had, perhaps commenting on their beauty and magnificence. And Jesus turned to them and said: "You see all these, do you not? Truly, I say to you, there will not be left here one stone upon another, that will not be thrown down" (24:2, RSV). His prediction was fulfilled in AD 70 when Jerusalem and the Temple were completely leveled to the ground, never to be restored to the magnificence they had seen earlier.

We have been going through a long period in which some of our theologians have talked about the silence of God in judgment on human society in terms of "God is dead." Yes, we heard a lot about the "Death of God theology" for a while and it was much misunderstood. Then came the "born-again" movement in which He seemed to be speaking again but not as effectively as He has spoken at other times because we have become so very tolerant in what we call our pluralistic society.

From the experience I have been having this past week in dealing with the flagrant pornography coming through on cable TV in particular, I am beginning to realize that something very radical must surely take place at some time down the road in expressing the displeasure of God against the forces that deal in the corrupting of the human spirit, exalting perversions of every kind in the sexual realm, encouraging violence as the basic action of living, and militating against the common good of the community and the integrity of family life.

I was given the assignment on the Mayor's Commission on Cable TV to write a policy statement in regard to programming for the issuing authority report. When I submitted it, the cable TV company representatives jumped on it and tried to tell us that it was illegal and that such a statement would be censorship, that the Supreme Court would in any court action surely strike down as they have before. For a while I felt like a lone voice as the others on the commission gingerly approached it. They have adopted it with the hope that we can clarify it and keep it as legal as possible when we vote on the final approval of the whole report.

At the same time, the newspapers were flooding us with reports about *Playboy* magazine developing a network for cable with "soft-core porn." Others were saying that "hard-core porn" has come into its own as that which the public wants and is clamoring to pay for in cable TV. The cable companies in many instances have policies of keeping X-rated material off their operations. But they are concerned that they may be losing huge profits because of the big money "porn" can command. The almighty dollar is "God," whether they will admit it or not.

It is interesting to note in our Old Testament lesson that God got radical in spelling out His will in no uncertain terms in the giving of the Ten Commandments. And in the giving of those Commandments, He singles out two for the most comment, namely the one having to do with "no other gods" and "sabbath rest." Long ago, God called Abraham out of just such a decadent society as we see ourselves in today, promising to make out of him a people set apart. God gave Abraham no rules. God just asked Abraham to follow His leading. But as the people grew in number and ended up suffering the cruelty of Egyptian rule so that He had to deliver them out of that bondage,

God found that He had to spell out His radical will in no uncertain terms for them.

That summary of His will in the Ten Commandments, which Martin Luther indicated is central to the Christian life by placing it first in his catechism, must again hold forth its radical character for our day. Without them, you and I cannot know or understand the fullness of the gospel's implications. They were intended not as threats but as ten easy to follow steps for the smooth running of God's specific society of His chosen people. To be sure, we have failed to measure up and need the gospel of forgiveness in the face of our failures, but we need to be more concerned with the implications of the law for the living of our life in Christian freedom.

When you buy a new car, a manual usually accompanies it in which the manufacturer tries to assist the owner in keeping the car in good running condition. Directions such as "Lubricate every ten thousand miles" are not intended to shame or frighten the owners, but to inform them. The factory which has built and tested the car is passing on information that is necessary to the life of the car. So the Ten Commandments are necessary for the life of a human being created in the image of God. God handed them down as a manual containing the ten easy steps to follow for the smooth maintenance of a growing nation of His people.

Knowing how His created beings worked as a whole and as parts, God does the radical thing, revealing to them His radical will for their very existence. They are radical because they get back to the roots of their very being in the first place. Originally this was all inscribed and implanted in their hearts, but this was soon crowded out by the thorns and thistles of self-centeredness, self-gratification, and the whole "mankind-come-of-age" syndrome which present-day humanists and liberals hold forth so strongly. What we are saying today is that *we* are gods and that nobody is going to censor what I can or cannot do, what I can or cannot view, but *nobody* ! We are gods who are free to determine for ourselves what we want.

It is just here that God comes in saying radically: "I am God and there is no other." You won't even try to make a picture or image of Me because I just can't be reproduced by you without that becoming a god for you. And as Israel from that starting point slowly began to read this human manual, they began to understand the nature of reality. They saw how sacred even His name was and the need for a sabbath rest. Then they were made aware of how they had to interrelate to others in the human family. Something was there about family life, about male-female interactions, and the use of the material things provided for the living out of our time on this earth. And as the radical meaning came through, they realized the great blessings of these instructions. Just read Psalm 19, beginning at verse 7, and you will get the flavor of their response: "The law of the Lord is perfect, reviving the soul . . ."(RSV).

Somehow we have allowed ourselves to take our Christian freedom and turn it into what I would term Christian license in ignoring these Ten Commandments in much of mainline denominational Christianity, including Lutheranism, today. I think of Donald Nichol's statement in his book *Holiness* about the freedom, no, about the license we take in observing the sabbath. He wrote:

> They say, with an air of wisdom, "But the Sabbath was made for man and not man for the sabbath." They misguidedly imagine that the quotation means that it is up to them to decide how they will use "their time" on the Sabbath. Whereas, in fact, the scriptural quotation means the opposite: that the sabbath is precisely God's time, a pause for the sake of man, decided upon by God, a period

when man has to stop working, worrying, and planning, when he must let go all of those activities and instead, be still, simply rejoicing in the presence of God. The fact that so many people pervert the scriptural quotation about the Sabbath, making it mean the opposite of what it says, only goes to indicate how deeply resistant man is to accepting the lesson that the institution of the Sabbath is intended to teach—and how very firm and strict one has to be with oneself, therefore, in observing the Sabbath discipline.

*The Lutheran* recently had an article on the Third Commandment which is written as if one were walking on eggs in not wanting to be legalistic in the least about it, while trying to say it's a good thing. The Boston Athletic Association came out in the newspapers this week declaring that the churches in Hopkinton were not justified in coming out against their decision to move the Boston Marathon to Sunday in 1984 rather than sit down with them and work out some kind of a compromise in regard to their firm decision to have it on Sunday. What kind of warped thinking that is!

When God gets radical, goes to the root of things, we had better begin to read carefully and take to heart what His instruction book says for living the free life that is ours in Christ. It is a freedom under His law which I often see my Jewish brothers and sisters understanding better than many who call themselves Christians. The radical new existence that is ours by faith in the gospel embodies life lived by the guidance of the Ten Commandments. Luther knew this as he wrote the Catechism, even though many modern-day Lutherans, as well as other Christians, seem to think this is a legalism that must be scrapped as undue censorship through the use of the morals of a past day. I often hear individuals say that the Ten Commandments were given for an agrarian society and they just don't apply to the kind of urban society we have today. That kind of thinking is just so much unadulterated baloney.

Unless you and I truly seek to embody the radical Ten Commandments into our life-style, it seems to me that it would be almost untenable to claim that our life is lived in Christ. Is that being too judgmental? Well, then, so be it. Christ is the new model to be sure. He did emphasize love of God and love of fellow persons as a summary of those Ten Commandments, but in so doing He did not abrogate the specifications laid down in those Ten Commandments. These specifications He incorporated and made full in that one four-letter word *love*.

# 8
# The Sabbath—the Lord's Day

Samuel A. Cartledge

God worked for six days in bringing His world to completion. Then on the seventh day God rested. That day of rest after six days of work has set an example for all of God's children. The sabbath is no new invention; it goes back to the very beginning.

When God gave His Ten Commandments to Moses on Mount Sinai, the Fourth Commandment made plain that God expected His children to keep the sabbath day. The word *sabbath* comes from the Hebrew word for rest, and rest from labor is an integral part of the observance of that day. But the Commandment makes it plain that God also expects us to use that day as a special day of worship; we are to keep it holy.

The keeping of the sabbath from that time forward has been a most distinctive feature of Judaism. And it is so to this very day in modern Israel.

But from early times it was recognized that there were problems as to how the sabbath should be kept. The positive side, keeping the day holy, would include such things as attendance of the worship services in the synagogues, times for special study of the Word of God, prayer, and meditation—things for which time would be available which would not be true on the days of regular work. The negative side, though, created far more problems. Man is not to work on that day of rest. But it can be immediately seen that it is absolutely impossible to refrain from all work on that day. The most primitive civilizations would require at least some work to keep people alive. So the concept of works of necessity arose early.

But what are works of necessity? Every one who seeks to keep the Commandment must try to find an answer to that question. As time went on, Jewish scholars sought to answer that question for every conceivable situation that could be imagined. They carried on their studies at such great length that they developed two large volumes. The Tractate Sabbath in the Talmud, I personally have read from beginning to the end! Much of it is very fine and reasonable, but some of it goes to absurd extremes.

In cold weather a fire is necessary. It is permitted to add fuel to a fire started before the sabbath. But if the fire goes out on the sabbath, a Jew must not do the work to start it again. He must either freeze, or get a Gentile friend to start it for him. Let the Gentile be the sinner!

When a Jew has a cold he needs to have his handkerchief. But it is illegal work to carry it in a pocket; it must be carried wrapped around the wrist.

And so we might go on and on and on.

When we come to the New Testament, we remember that Jesus Himself had disputes with the Jewish scholars of His day about the keeping of the sabbath. They accused Him of breaking the sabbath. But did He?

Remember Matthew 5:17-18:

> Think not that I have come to abolish the law and the prophets; I have come not to abolish them but to fulfil them. For truly, I say to you, till heaven and earth pass away, not an iota, not a dot, will pass from the law until all is accomplished (RSV).

Does that sound like a lawbreaker? We see Jesus regularly attending the worship in the synagogue. He re-

frained from ordinary work. He never broke God's law,
but He did not hesitate to violate man's traditional interpretation of the law when He was convinced that that
interpretation violated the true spirit of the law itself.

Jesus' disciples were going through a grain field on the
sabbath. They satisfied their hunger by feeding themselves from the grain. The Jewish scholars accused them
of breaking the law. They were not stealing; the law allowed hungry people to satisfy their hunger by taking
food from the field. But the scholars accused them of work
by running a mill when they rubbed their hands together
to remove the chaff!

Jesus healed a woman who had had an infirmity for
eighteen years on the sabbath. He was condemned as a
breaker of the law. Of course a physician could heal on the
sabbath only in cases of life and death, when it was probable that the patient would not live unless treated on the
sabbath. This woman had been living with her infirmity
for eighteen years, so it was not probably that she would
die if not healed on the sabbath. The same thing was true
when Jesus healed a man with a withered hand in the
synagogue on the sabbath, and also when He told a healed
man to take up his bed and go home healed. A strict
interpretation of the Jewish tradition was not in accord
with the true interpretation of God's law. Jesus' acts of
healing did not keep Him or His patients from performing
what the Fourth Commandment required. He would not
allow His love to be limited by a false tradition.

The apostles and the early followers of Jesus continued
to keep the true provisions of the sabbath law. They regularly attended the worship services of the synagogue. On
all of his missionary journeys, Paul went to the synagogues
to worship and to preach to the assembled Jews about
Jesus as their Messiah.

But it was on the first day of the week that God raised

His crucified Son from the dead. For the Christians, that resurrection of Jesus was recognized as even more important than God's resting from His creative work on the seventh day. As the Jews became less numerous in the Christian church and the Gentiles became more and more numerous, the Christians began to celebrate the Lord's Day on the first day of the week.

We must admit that we can point to no direct command that we cease observing the seventh day and begin using the first day. But there are several passages that indicate rather clearly that the early Christians were using the first day as their day of special rest and worship. Acts 20:7: "On the first day of the week, when we were gathered together to break bread, Paul talked with them" (RSV). 1 Corinthians 16:2: "On the first day of every week, each of you is to put something aside and store it up" (RSV), evidently referring to the weekly collection at the time of worship. Revelation 1:10: "I was in the Spirit on the Lord's Day" (RSV), probably refers to the Christian Lord's Day, though some scholars refer it to the eschatological Day of the Lord.

When we pass the time of the New Testament, the earliest tradition makes it clear that the first day of the week was the Christians' holy day. In the medieval lectionaries, sabbath was used for Saturday lessons, while the Lord's Day was used for the Sunday ones. And there is almost universal agreement (except for the Seventh-Day Adventists) that Christians should keep the first day of the week, the Lord's Day, as their holy day of the week.

But how should we Christians observe our Lord's Day? The Fourth Commandment is still a part of the law of God. Those of us who have been saved by grace through faith should still seek to keep the law as we strive to make of ourselves good children of our Heavenly Father. We

72911

still love the law of God and seek to discover how it would have us live acceptably to God.

We changed the day of the week from the seventh to the first, but it is still one day in seven. We seek to understand the true spirit of the law of the sabbath, striving to learn from the good things of Jewish tradition and especially from the teachings and actions of Jesus Himself. We can learn from the writings and actions of our fellow Christians of previous times and our own time; the fellowship of the saints can mean much to us here.

Jesus taught us that the sabbath was made for mankind and not mankind for the sabbath, and we should take that seriously. Some lightly and falsely use this to try to justify throwing away all restrictions and making this day just like all the other days of the week. Of course, Jesus never meant anything like that. Surely He meant to teach us that God gave us the sabbath as a wonderfully fine gift for our good. Surely we do not need to justify the benefits to us of having a regular day of rest for our bodies. Nor do we as Christians have to justify the benefits of having a special day of worship and spiritual enrichment. God has given us this wonderful day, and each of us should seek to make the very best possible use of it.

Living in a pluralistic society and believing in the separation of church and state, we must seek to avoid trying to get the state to pass laws forcing others to worship as Christians. No law of the state can ever force anyone to worship God as a Christian or in any other way. At the most, we can seek to have laws that will grant the opportunity of a day of rest and worship for those who choose to use it.

The old Jewish sabbath was a wonderful day, but the Christian Lord's Day incorporates all of that with the added glory of remembering the resurrection of our Lord and all that that has meant for us. Surely we and our children should look upon it as the best of all the days of the whole week, truly enjoying its rest and its opportunities of the finest and most meaningful worship of our Heavenly Father, who on this day brought life and immortality to us through our Lord's victory over sin and death. And may this Lord's Day here on earth be a foretaste of that Day of the Lord when we shall live throughout all eternity in the very presence of the Lord.

# 9
# The Lord's Day

*Acts 20:7; 1 Corinthians 16:2; Revelation 1:10*

**by Welton C. Gaddy**

Recent revisions of those ancient laws related to business operations on Sunday have provoked multiple reactions. Some people have happily heralded the changes as optimistic signs that our society has finally come of age. Other persons, more despondently, have made the legislative acts analogous to fiery darts shot by Satan into the soul of contemporary Christianity. Numerous additional responses dot the continuum between these two extremes. Most everyone holds some kind of opinion. Few individuals have remained totally silent.

As a preacher-pastor, I have felt keenly a responsibility to speak to the changed situation. Quite honestly, my preparation in this regard was characterized by a methodology which was faulty. In the beginning, I isolated certain key points which I wanted to make. Then, I turned to the Scriptures in order to discover a foundation for my thoughts and validation for my emphases. Of course, such an approach to the Bible is totally out of order. Holy Scripture is read not from a posture of open-minded study but from the perspective of a prejudiced search for the kind of texts needed to prove particular points.

Thankfully, the revelation of God in the Bible challenged and corrected the false assumptions of my previous deliberation. As I struggled with various biblical texts,

I realized that the teachings of the Bible did not corre-
spond with my thinking or support all of my opinions. A
moment arrived when I had to decide either to forego a
reliance upon biblical authority and address the subject of
Sunday observance out of my own personal feelings or to
reexamine my position on the matter in the light of biblical revelation, make appropriate alterations, and then develop the content of my proclamation. This sermon
represents a serious attempt at the second approach.

Sunday observance by Christians has been shaped by a
most interesting history. It all started with another day of
the week in a religion other than Christianity. To trace
this history involves a trek through Holy Scripture, but
also investigation outside the biblical revelation.

In Old Testament thought, the seventh day of the week
—our Saturday—was considered and called the sabbath.
One of the Ten Commandments offers the stern warning
that this day must be kept holy. Both from within the
Decalogue and from other passages in the Old Testament,
it is obvious that when religious leaders addressed the
matter of how to keep the day holy, they described the
sabbath essentially as a day of rest. God's rest on the seventh day of creation was made the prototype for Sabbath
observance among all people. Elaborate, to the point of
ridiculous, regulations were established so that work
could be avoided and rest practiced.

Worship on the sabbath—the sabbath as a day of worship—was a later emphasis predicated upon the belief
that no completely satisfying rest can occur apart from
worship. Within Judaism, detailed definitions of rest were
joined to prolific warnings about work in a stringent effort
to protect the sanctity of the day. The sabbath became a
primal institution in Jewish religion. Sabbath observance
was considered an unparalleled act of religious devotion.

Such was the situation when Jesus embarked upon His mission.

Following the earthly ministry of Jesus, after His resurrection and ascension, most of the early Christians, who were Jews, continued the worship patterns of their life-long faith. Naturally, then, the sabbath, Saturday, remained their day of worship. This practice was altered when the Christian gospel was accepted in the Graeco-Roman world. In this new context, people were not committed to an observance of the Old Testament sabbath by means of adherence to the multiple Jewish regulations. In fact, many early Christians viewed the Fourth Commandment of the Decalogue as a ceremonial part of the law now abrogated and transcended by Christ. Thus, members of the primitive community of faith began to worship on the day of the week on which the resurrection of the Lord had occurred, the same day on which Jesus had first appeared in the midst of His disciples (Luke 24:1-9; John 20:19*ff*). Sunday was to be the day of worship. Sunday worship was considered a weekly celebration of the resurrection. Sunday was to be the Lord's Day.

In the singular emphasis in Sunday observance focused on worship. Sunday was a day of worship. In reality, Sunday was not a day of rest and could not be a day of rest because Sunday was a regular work day in the Graeco-Roman world. Typically, Christians fulfilled their business obligations during the daylight hours of a Sunday, meeting together for worship either very early in the morning or very late in the evening. Late-night services usually included a fellowship meal, worship centered around the Lord's Supper, and proclamation of the Word of God.

Apparently such a Sunday evening service was the occasion described in Acts 20. Notice in that passage the writer's specific reference to the lateness of the hour. According to the biblical text, Paul prolonged his sermon to the extent that a man named Eutychus went to sleep and fell out the window. Of course, it takes neither a post-workday Sunday evening worship service nor an inordinately long sermon to induce a similar type of ecclesiastical slumber, even today!

Sunday worship at early and late hours continued to be the Christian's method of observing the Lord's Day for a number of years. In the fourth century, specifically in the year AD 321, the Emperor Constantine made Sunday a public holiday. Constantine's decision was not motivated by Christian conviction. Rather, the emperior's concern related to a proper observance of "the most honorable day of the sun." No matter. At long last, Christians could rest and worship on the same day. The Lord's Day was a day of worship by spiritual decree and a day of rest by political-legal decree.

As Christians began to adjust to this changed situation, they began to see the Lord's Day—already a day of worship—as a new kind of sabbath, a day of rest. Most scholars agree that the first equation of Sunday and sabbath within the church came at this point in the fourth century. In order to provide for worshipers some basic guidelines for a proper observance of the Lord's Day, regulations from the Old Testament sabbath observance were appropriated and applied to the New Testament Sunday. Strangely enough, though, contemporary views of Sunday observance have been constructed primarily on the basis of this biblically untenable equation rather than on material in the biblical revelation.

Presently, we find ourselves in a situation forcing once more a reevaluation of the meaning and significance of Sunday. Just as before, a reconsideration of Sunday observances has been prompted more by legal action than by an interest in biblical instruction. The end result of the entire matter remains in question. Perhaps Sunday no longer will be viewed as a day of rest. That is debatable. However, whether or not Sunday is considered a day of worship is unrelated to legislative action or to cultural persuasion. Status for some matters transcends majority voices and popular choices. Make no mistake about it, the intentions of God Almighty and the laws of civil government can never be made synonymous. Human decisions, whether in the halls of legislatures or in the living rooms of homes, do not revoke biblical injunctions. Sunday is a day of worship. That issue was settled long ago.

Perhaps by now I have raised more questions than I have provided answers. Some confusion could exist. You may be wondering where I actually stand in regard to the numerous legislative revisions and societal alterations which have affected the status of Sunday in our communities. Do I favor the new situation in which Sunday virtually is disregarded as a unique day either for rest or for worship? No, by no means. However, the basis of my response to that question is broader than a concern for Sunday observance alone.

Do I like what has happened to Sunday in our society? No! I am not pleased with the kind of rabid commercialism in our communities which seeks to squeeze work from every waking moment of its employees and coins from its customers. While I favor equitable laws—laws more reflective of the provisions of the United States Constitution—in relation to Sunday, I fervently oppose the "business as usual" attitude of the economic community. Remember that none of the revisions in legislation related to Sunday observance requires the full-scale operation of business establishments. A gross gnawing in our economic stomachs betrays the kind of unhealthy hunger that can be satisfied only at the expense of a loss of life in both patient and doctor.

My answer is no because I am not pleased with commu-

nity leaders who completely ignore the spiritual dimen-
sion of life. Providing for persons, caring for people,
whether by a father for members of his family or by a
community for its citizenry, involves far more than a
ready availability of material goods. Any realistic view of
personhood takes cognizance of people's spiritual needs
as well as their physical needs. A sometimes medical
professor at Harvard has even gone so far as to list worship
as one of the four essentials of life. Good providers,
whether individuals or institutions, take into account the
needs of the human spirit.

Please do not misunderstand. Personally, I have no
desire to impose my particular religious beliefs and practices upon anyone else—whether by legislation or by
some other means. However, in a spiritually undernour-
ished society, efforts which erode even more the possibility for spiritual nurture are worthy of protest. A blatant
disregard for the significance of Sunday exposes a debas-
ing view of personhood which strikes a blow at human
health. As one wise individual commented, "Without God
a man cannot bear the burden of himself."

My answer is no because I am disturbed by the trend
toward community disintegration of which numerous recent alterations in Sunday observance constitute only a
part. At what point in time do residents of a community
rest? Anyone who sits in a place of counsel, listening and
observing as individuals, families, and organizations come
apart at the seams, knows that communal rest is despa-
rately needed. A community which chooses to ignore the
significance of Sunday observance opts to increase the
possibility of even greater fragmentation among its citizenry, especially among its families. No doubt, local
churches will be expected to pick up the remains and put
them back together.

My answer is no because I am disturbed at the elimination of an authentic symbol of the sanctity of time and of the necessity of faith. In the past, Sunday stood as a reminder that all time is sacred and that all of life is to be lived by faith. When that symbol of remembrance has been diminished completely, one does not have to ponder long what will go next.

During my years at The Southern Baptist Theological Seminary in Louisville, Kentucky, most weekdays were spent in the city. However, weekends were spent in a different community where my student pastorate was located. Thus, our family was never in Louisville except at times when stores were open and streets were full. Shortly after graduating from the seminary and accepting a pastorate in Louisville, an interesting conversation took place on the way home from worship one Sunday morning. Having never before seen all of the shopping districts in the city closed during daylight hours, our oldest son raised the question of why. He did not understand the absence of activity. I explained to him the societal recognition of Sunday which existed at that time. We talked about Sunday in relation to personal needs for rest and worship. Sadly, today that kind of conversation would not be prodded by the context established by most communities. No longer will most children be able to note any distinctives related to Sunday activities. What have we done? In destroying the uniqueness of the day, are we not silencing its symbolic witness and, thus, hushing some of the most important questions related to the kind of holy life to which Sunday once quietly pointed?

Do I like what has happened to Sunday in our society? No. But that is not the whole story.

As a result of altered legislation and adjusted business practices on Sunday, Christians are now in a position to be more responsible in our worship and more authentic in our witness. In reality, new laws have not changed the nature of the day for us; they only have changed the possibilities for our observance of that day. Our current position is very similar to that of Christians prior to the fourth century. We are now a minority in a somewhat irreverent society. Worship is no longer the only activity available on a Sunday morning. Numerous alternatives to church attendance exist. The very laws about which so many have despaired have freed us to demonstrate even more effectively the importance of Sunday in our lives.

Actually, people should not attend church services because stores are closed, but because they want to worship God. Individuals should not forego golf for worship on a Sunday because golf courses are closed, but because, loving God more than golf, they choose to worship. Sunday-related legislation which disturbs many people serves to provide for us an uneasy freedom—freedom in which we can demonstrate worship born not out of habit or convenience but out of commitment.

To be sure, neither any other person nor I really can dictate how people should spend their Sundays. Personally, I have no interest or competence sufficient to judge your decisions in that regard. However, I can assure you that the divinely inspired Word of God in the New Testament conveys the intent that Sunday be used for worship —not because it is the sabbath, but because it is the Lord's Day. Keep in mind, as well, that He to whom the day belongs is the One to whom ultimately we are responsible in our observance of it. Sunday is the Lord's Day!

# 10
# Remember the Sabbath Day

*Exodus 20:8*

by John D. Scott, Sr.

"[Earnestly] remember the sabbath day, to keep it holy [withdrawn from common employment and dedicated to God]" (Ex. 20:8, AMP).

In our responsive reading entitled, "The Ten Commandments" (Ex. 20:1-17), about halfway through, the instruction concerning observance of the sabbath can be found. The board of directors of The Lord's Day League of New England has recommended that the Sunday after Easter be used to proclaim the concerns of that League. Whether or not I was a member of that board, I would want to give this cause my earnest attention.

From *The Amplified Bible,* we learn that we need to withdraw from "common" labor on this one-day-a-week occasion. While most of us are in full agreement with this injunction, let me repeat, at the very beginning of this message, that the words of instruction for the observance are simple—*rest* and *worship*!

While it may be beneficial to reiterate the Old Testament instruction (and I do not mean to neglect that aspect) I want to examine with you some of the historically American aspects of sabbath observance.

From our earliest days as a colony, the concern for the proper observance of the sabbath has been a way of life. From our modern-day standpoint, some of the restrictions from that day seem oppressive, but none can deny that there was a day set aside from the ordinary activity for rest and worship. Only acts of necessity were countenanced, such as care for domestic animals. Food was prepared on Saturday. Fire was lit for warmth only. All wood had been split the day before. And rest, with worship, was the order of the day.

If there were those who disagreed with this observance, they were nonvocal for the most part. As can be noted in the Word, certain emergency-type activities were acceptable. However, since the very term "emergency" begs for acceptable definition, some folk could find ways to skirt the law.

In my study for this message, I was reminded of some changes that have taken place in my lifetime. In my earlier years, places of business were closed on Sunday. Manufacture came to a standstill on Saturday evening. Secular activity on Sunday was kept to a minimum. Family gatherings and church activity were the main events. (I know that it must sound like I really did come from the dark ages!)

When our nation began to gear up for World War II, when the young men of our country went off to military training camps, the labor force was drastically diminished. The need for increased production became evident. With our government's encouragement, our business went to a seven-day week. Factories began to operate twenty-four hours a day, with workers on the job for a minimum forty-eight hours a week. In the heat of the battle to maintain military supremacy, sabbath observance became just one more matter that "must" be put aside in the interest of national defense.

While I have purposely simplified that era, the matter that is the focus of my thought remains vital. The need for relaxation was soon the proclaimed doctrine. Days off came in midweek. Sundays became double-time days.

With money becoming more an issue, those who refused to work on Sundays became a minority. The almighty dollar ruled.

While the fervency of that day ran at a fever pitch, there were some who refused to be swayed. One company in our area refused to work a seven-day-a-week schedule. They opened their mill with the day shift on Monday morning. They closed their week with a ten-hour day on Saturday, divided between their two working shifts. From reports with which I am familiar, that company had less absenteeism, experienced less mechanical breakdowns, and enjoyed a high production rate.

With the end of the war, there was the expressed desire to return to normalcy. But our economy had become so geared to mass production that factory work continued seven days a week. People still felt the need for recreation, and Sunday was the logical day.

While we really have not been at war for all of these years, the world has been in constant conflict. We have continued our mad rush for relaxation, recreation, and leisure time. Modern industry has become computerized and our "free time" has been increased. Sundays have become the favorite day for sports activity. First of all, major sports became acceptable on Sundays. In the rush for relaxation, family outings with picnics and pick-up sports games became acceptable. Next came the planned youth activities—what better day than Sunday? So, we have our Sunday Little Leagues, our games of all kinds, on Sunday. Hockey rinks that stay open twenty-four hours a day, seven days a week, place some teams on practice schedule on Sunday, during the usual church worship hour.

In Massachusetts, Sunday of a recent year would have been the date of the Boston Marathon, if it had not been for the church leaders in nearby Hopkinton. We are fast becoming a non-Christian nation, and we can mark its beginnings with the relaxation of rest and worship on the Lord's Day!

While a review of history, brief of necessity, cannot be used as an excuse for the neglect of the sabbath observance, it seemed important. The Church of the Nazarene has always championed sabbath observance. In some areas, we probably were considered to be real "radicals" on this matter, but so be it!! As recently as our 1980 General Assembly in Dallas, Texas, the manual revision committee gave the sabbath-observance admonition strong support.

Under the General Rules, paragraph 26, on pages 37-40, are included these words, "All who desire to unite with the Church of the Nazarene . . . show evidence of salvation from their sins by godly walk. . . . They shall evidence their commitment to God—FIRST. By doing that which is enjoined in the Word of God." Then there is an enumeration of seven matters, with scriptural references, each dealing with matters of positive activity. That article continues on page 39 with words, "SECOND. By avoiding evil of every kind, including, . . ." and a list follows, covering eight areas of concern.

I am interested in Number 2. Avoid "Profaning of the Lord's Day by participation in unnecessary secular activities, thereby indulging in practices which deny its sanctity." Following this statement is a list of Bible references. Heading that list is our Scripture portion for this message. Then comes God's promise to sabbath observers in Isaiah 58:13-14; Christ's words in Mark 2:27-28 that He is Lord of the sabbath; Acts 20:7 where the church in Troas met on Sunday to "break bread" and hear Paul preach; and Revelation 1:10 where John notes that he was "in the Spirit" when God spoke to him "on the Lord's Day."

Let me point out that such verses are not exhaustive.

Admonitions for sabbath observance are found through-out God's Word.

For us to acquiesce to the pressures of our day, and to become a part of all the recreational activity that is now reserved for Sundays, is to deny God's sovereignty.

I would like to challenge each one of you to do a person-al survey of your attitude toward God's day. How much time do you give to the attitude of worship? How many of you use the day for rest only, neglecting worship, just so that you may be at your best for the secular employer on Monday? You would never think to take a day off from "work" so that you could be better rested for worship, but we seem to have little compunction about the reverse.

Perhaps our major problem is that we simply do not think. Instead, we act and react. Our weariness becomes overbearing. We see no real need for a sabbath of rest and worship, only one of rest!

Let us take another look at this Commandment, and "[Earnestly] remember the sabbath day, to keep it holy [withdrawn from common employment and dedicated to God]" (Ex. 20:8).

# 11
# Remember the Sabbath Day

*Exodus 20*

**by William L. Self**

I like the story that Cecil Meyers tells of the massive expedition into the heart of the darkest jungles of Africa. The men were anxious to get to the place they wanted to go because there seemed to be great treasure there, and the expedition that looked somewhat like a scene out of a Tarzan movie with the great white hunters up front and the African men carrying the burdens pressed hard every day. Finally, after they had pressed on and on, day after day, the laborers refused to carry the burdens. When asked why, the Africans' response was, "You've pressed us too hard. We want to rest, wait, and let our souls catch up with our bodies."

I think that's a parable of us in our modern day. Somehow along the way we have gotten the confusion of God's gift of the sabbath mixed up with all kinds of rules and regulations having to do with the sabbath. God gave us a great day, "This is the day that the Lord hath made" (Ps. 118:24). God made a day and gave it to us for one reason— He made us in His own image. The Bible says that it took God six days to create the world and then He rested. God created us like unto Himself and He created us in such a way that after a period of work and stress, we need to have a time of refurbishing, a time of rekindling in the inner person. So God created the sabbath.

We're going to talk about which day, how to use it, and

the fact that God never intended for the sabbath day to be a burden. You recall the incident in the life of Jesus when He was caught in a sabbath controversy. He was so disgusted with the way the sabbath had been weighed with rules and regulations that He said that mankind was not created for the sabbath, the sabbath was created for mankind.

I love the church in which I grew up. It's a great church. It gave me my spiritual roots. I found Jesus Christ as Savior and Lord there and answered His call to preach, so I could never say anything negative about it. But I remember in those early days the great issue in our church was whether or not one could be a Christian and go to a movie on Sunday afternoon. That seems to be a faraway problem today. We've long since passed that. But the only thing to do in our little town was either go to the beach, go to the movie, or get into trouble.

So, we'd sit around and debate those things all the time. The very conservative would say that not only can you not go on Sunday afternoon, you shouldn't even go on Saturday night. The liberals would say that maybe you could go if you'd been a good boy all week, or something like that. At some point, a great compromise was worked out that seemed to satisfy everybody. You could go to the movie on Sunday afternoon, if you would be out in time for Training Union!

In the whole process, we get caught up in all these rules and regulations. The Hebrew took the great gift of the sabbath, labeled it, and watered it down with so many regulations that a person could hardly move. Did you know that a woman was forbidden to look into a mirror on the sabbath? The reasoning was that if she did, she would probably see a gray hair and if she saw a gray hair, she would pluck it out. Plucking out a gray hair was work. If a man with a wooden leg was caught in a house that was burning on the sabbath, he could run outside, but he couldn't pick up his wooden leg, for that would be carrying something on the sabbath day. This is an actual legislative procedure out of the old sabbath code and, of course, it's ridiculous.

I remember years ago Billy Graham was preaching in London and took some time away before the crusade was to begin to walk through the woods on Sunday. A group of people who were strict Sabbatarians wrote him a very strong criticism because he spent some time walking through the woods on the sabbath day.

Now we have these extremes and because of that many of us have moved away from any kind of strict Sunday observance. Then we get into the Blue Laws. Do you know why they're called "Blue Laws?" They came out of a Massachusetts book, a civil code, written up on how Sunday was to be observed. There were all these picky little regulations about what you could and could not do, which had come from our Puritan background. They were put in a book with a blue cover, so when they were attacked, they were referred to as the book with the blue cover, or the Blue Laws. (That's just a little side information.)

We're living in a day of stress. I see it all the time. If there has ever been a day in the history of the world that has had greater stress, I don't know when it was. I see marriages breaking up, I see people who are totally disintegrated, I see people who are caught up with alcohol and drugs, I see people who cannot live under the stress of life without constant depression. Depression has become one of the major medical problems in the United States today. I don't know all the reasons. We could probably come up with some fancy ones, but I know one thing: God didn't intend for people to be this way.

God built people not to be this way, and God built into

the fiber of the universe, as well as the fiber of our lives, a way for us not to be this way. He gave us a sabbath. He gave us a day to stop and to let things come together again. He gave us a day when we can blow the whistle on life and say that we aren't going to destroy the inner person anymore because we're going to be the man or woman who is committed to re-creating what we are inside, what God intended for us to be. We need to stop and let our spirit and soul catch up with our body. Longfellow said that the sabbath is the golden clasp that holds the pages of the week together. I think he was right.

## Sabbath or Sunday—Which Day?

I know now why God called me to that little church in Florida when I was in college. It's been the source of illustration through the years. If He hadn't called me there, I wouldn't have had anything to talk about. For those of you who are new with us, I was the associate pastor of the First Baptist Church of Palatka, Florida, and later I was the mission pastor of that church and did both jobs on the weekends when I was at Stetson University. When I was the associate pastor, my job was to take a group of young people down to the county jail for services on Sunday afternoons.

The jail looked at that time like something out of a Burt Reynolds movie. The people were those who had been picked up at the honky tonks and bars all around the town and had been brought into the county jail to spend the weekend. You can imagine the kind of clientele we had in "church." This was in the 1950s, so the black men and the white men were separated, as were the white and black women. We made our way to each division of cells and had services. One day, we came to one of the men's sections and I was preaching as best I could. The guys were playing their dice game down on the floor and finally one man said, "Wait a minute, preacher, I want to ask you a question."

Well, I got so excited because I thought he had actually been listening to my sermon. He said, "I want to know what day you should go to church." There was a guy locked up on Sunday afternoon and he wanted to know what day he was supposed to go to church! So, I stopped and got into the sabbath question with him, and like any college sophomore would do, I gave him a fifteen-minute recitation about the sabbath and Sunday and it sounded like a term paper ready to be turned in to the professor. He just smiled and my time was up. The sheriff came and ushered us out. I realized what the fellow had done. He didn't want to hear the gospel, he just wanted to get me off the gospel and onto something that didn't touch him where he was. I'd been doing it in class for years, but I had never had it happen to me in a preaching service.

A lot of people have used Sunday that way. But God created us a holy people. It was a holy situation—then He gave a holy day. This holy day is significant. It was a day of rejoicing, it was a gift of God to people, it was a day when was to have everything stopped. It was a day of no work. The word *sabbath* does not mean seven, it means cessation, the quitting of work. Everything stopped on that day. When you stop everything, if you just throw a switch and close down life, then everybody can begin to let things come together.

Today in the Arab section of Jerusalem on the sabbath day there is business and commerce, but in the Jewish section almost everything is boarded up, completely closed down. There are times that you're not to go through these sections on the sabbath because it's a violation of the sabbath, and there is strong feeling against anyone who would violate it. I strongly believe the reason the Jewish people have endured so many hardships through the years is because of their tough-minded adherence to the sabbath.

The early Christians were obsessed with the fact that they came out of a Jewish background and yet God had done something new to them, something real in the Easter experience. So they would have the sabbath experience, and then they would gather together as the Christian sect on Sunday morning and celebrate the resurrection.

In AD 321, Constantine, emperor of the Holy Roman Empire, said that Sunday would be our day of worship. It was reconfirmed in 782 when Charlemagne said the same thing. But there is a difference. The sabbath says, in effect, six days shalt thou labor—you work until you get to the sabbath and rest. You work toward it and rest. But Sunday is the day that gives you strength so that you can work the six days that are in front of you. One is at the end of the week, the other is at the beginning of the week. The sabbath is from sundown to sundown, but Sunday is from midnight to midnight. The sabbath is the seventh day, Sunday is the first day of the week. The sabbath is the day of rest, but Sunday is a day of worship. The sabbath has a penalty if you break it; Sunday has no penalty, except that you have shortchanged yourself.

The Christian, as I have already noted, draws his strength out of a worship experience on Sunday. It's more than a time to quit work, it's a time to let God talk to the inner person. It's a time when we make real that practice which says in effect, "Be still and know that I am God." It's an understanding, not legalism. Now the Christians took all the value out of the Hebrew sabbath and put into it the great joy of the Christian resurrection; so we have a marriage of the two in the Christian community.

## Holy Day or Holiday?

We're in a great holiday mood in America. I think the three-day weekend when we've moved George Washington's birthday and everybody else's birthday over to Monday is going to do more damage than we'll ever realize. The idea of moving things around to get the longer weekend is not helping us any. But I can stand in this pulpit until I have no breath or vocal cords left and decry the violence on the sabbath, the violent use of the sabbath, and I think all of us would agree, but we're caught in some kind of conveyor belt.

Some of you work in businesses where you have no control over what you do on Sunday. Some of you are managers of businesses where someone in a distant city makes the decisions and you're caught up in it. You can't get out of it and you don't know what to do. You know it's wrong, it violates everything you are, and you wonder how much you can give. Then we've run into the holiday attitude, and here I go again, forgive me, but this is just one of my little things. I really don't think that anyone is going to do much worshiping when all the athletic contests are held on God's day.

Now, I may be a closet Sabbatarian, I may have "blue laws" embedded into my veins, but I can't help it. I don't believe anything good is going to come out of that when you take all the people and turn them over to some kind of gladiatorial contest in the name of recreation. It's secular idolatry. You can go to any major city in America where major league athletics have come in and watch the the level of church attendance. The coming of major league athletics means that the churches start having trouble every time. It does something to Sunday. Thoreau said if you want to destroy the Christian faith, first take away Sunday. I think he was right in that particular insight. It's a holy day. For those of you who have gathered around the cross, have been saved and washed clean by His blood, it's a sacrilege to do anything else on that day except to celebrate what God has done.

What did He say in the Commandment, "Remember the sabbath day"? Let this be a time when you stop and remember what God has done. All the Hebrews would come together, and they would look back and remember what God had done as He brought them through the Red Sea and through all the troubles they had had. They remembered the hand of God in the feeding of the manna, the giving of the quail, the sweet waters of Elim, the parting of the Red Sea, the killing of Pharaoh. Oh, what a day of rejoicing that was as they celebrated what God had done.

Now we come together on the first day of the week. He did something for us. He broke open the tomb. He brought Jesus Christ out. He gives life. We come together as a body of Christ and remember what God has done. It's sacrament, it's done in remembrance of what Christ has done for us. How we've constructed today—morning worship and Bible study, evening training and worship—makes a day where the soul is rekindled. You may miss a dinner party, a trip out of town, or you may miss a trip to the beach, but you won't miss heaven. Your life won't disintegrate. It just depends on what you want to do.

A man came to me one day and said, "I'm old, I'm tired, I never cared much about church because I never had time for God. I've worked hard and it's too late for me now." I looked at him and said, "You've had four thousand Sundays in your adult life. What have you done with them?" Of course you have time for God. This is a day that reminds us that all things are His, as the tithe reminds us that all dollars are His. This is the day when we come aside to give the Highest a hearing.

## Use It or Abuse It?

OK, you agree that we take the value of the sabbath and put the resurrection on it and make it a special day. You agree that going against the grain of Sunday openings is going to make it harder. I have noticed that it's harder to baptize people now than it's ever been before because many of the prospects we're looking at and the people we're witnessing to are working on Sunday. Society has gotten caught up in a seven-day week, twenty-four hours a day. If you abuse Sunday you're going to destroy something beautiful that God has given. No Sunday means no church. No church means no worship; no worship, no religion; no religion, no morality; no morality, no society; no society, no government; no government—anarchy. That's the choice before you.

So, what do you do with the day? Do you sit around and read the Bible all day long? That might not be a bad idea for some of us. There are always those people who say, "I can worship God out on the golf course." I play golf and it isn't worship when I'm out there! Some of you will remember that I used to call those people who want to get out into God's great outdoors, God's great blue domers. They're going to worship under the blue dome out there.

That isn't worship, that's recreation. Worship is when you're with the body of Christ. Don't ever negate public worship, for something flows between us when we're here together. There is a great, intangible thing that moves among us. Those of you who are full give to those who are empty; those who are weak come to get their cups filled. God is here. God's presence is here among us, even though you don't hear thunder and lightning. May I suggest six ways to use the sabbath.

Worship—real worship is not optional. The tragedy of the modern church is we make worship an option. How many of you got up this morning and had to consciously make a decision to come to church today? How many of you are going to go home this afternoon and about 4:00 "decide" whether or not you're coming to church tonight? A Christian should never have to make that decision; it should be programmed into his life. I'll tell you one thing, we'd have a lot less chaos dealing with Christians if the Christians would worship. We'd have a lot less grumbling, less distress, less mental problems, less alcoholism if you'd just take what God has given you and worship.

Good conduct—it's a time when you should do things that are holy. I don't care how long you have to stand in gasoline lines, if you do a little planning, you don't have to do your shopping on Sunday. I remember one of the strong discussions we had at our house was whether or not one of the children should or should not buy some things on Sunday. It's old-fashioned, it's out-of-date, I'm not with it, I'm not swinging, but I decided we were not going to do our shopping on Sunday. There can be time to do things like that on other days. There is only so much money out there, you're going to divide it six ways or seven, but then I'm not a businessman.

Remember that every day is His. It's not "give Him one day and do as you please the other six."

Be aware of your witness. What about your neighbor? Can he set his clock by the fact that your car pulls out of the driveway at a certain time on Sunday morning and you're on your way to the worship of God. Or is it, "They're members of Wieuca Road Baptist Church when they go anywhere." We don't like for anyone to remind us of the power of our witness; we want to do our own thing. No man liveth unto himself, or dieth unto himself.

It's a day for family. I realize that a lot of families don't want this much time together. I realize that many families are caught up with working and strained schedules that don't fit into nice compartments like this sermon alludes to, but it needs to be a day for family, prayer, and thinking. However you handle it, walking in the woods, doing something together as a family, whatever, this should be done after you worship. Substituting family time for worship time is like having an automobile with the front end out of line. It's going to ultimately wear itself out.

You need to prepare for it. I doubt if there was much preparation this morning before you came to church. That isn't the way the Hebrew did; he spent a lot of time preparing for the sabbath. How many of you bothered to pray for the choir before you came? How many of you prayed for me before you came? How many of you prayed for your Sunday School teacher? I think the attitude is more like, "Let's see what they have for me today. It had better be good, because I could have gone to a ball game, played golf, or stayed home and read the paper." God blesses in relationship to our preparation.

This is the day of rejoicing, this is the day the Lord hath made. Take it as a gift from God and use it. It's not a burden to be imposed upon the people of God, but a joy. It's God's answer to the mental-health struggles of our day. This is God's great gift for us, it is a holy day when we will get strength for living. We have a special God who is not worshiped with idols. We have a special God whose Name is holy. We have a special God who has given us a holy day. Let us rejoice and be glad in it.

# 12

# Is the Battle Lost? or Thoughts on the Internalization of Principle

## by Stephen W. Nease

How well I remember in boyhood days the time when, after the Sunday family dinner was done, I left the house on the pretext of going for an "afternoon walk," but, by previous arrangement with my pal, Johnny, ended up at the "Old Ball Park."

When I returned home much later than a Sunday afternoon walk would take, and nearly late for the Sunday evening evangelistic service (as we used to call it), Mother met me at the door, her face set in that determined look that always told me when I was in trouble.

"Stephen Wesley, where have you been?" she asked. Now when my mother used both of my names I knew she knew my secret!

Knowing better than to compound my troubles by deceit, I responded, flippantly, "Well, Mother, Johnny and I decided to see the Legion team play at Merrymount Park this afternoon."

The roof caved in! The paddle came out! The Puritan's punishment of Thomas Morton and his crowd of revelers at Merrymount in bygone days was to me mere child's play compared to the wrath of my Christian mother that Sunday afternoon!

And somehow, in looking back, I'm kind of glad she stood for her convictions despite her only son's rebellion.

Oh, yes, we did get to that Sunday evening evangelistic

service. You guessed it—when the invitation was given, I led the way to the mourner's bench!

But enough reminiscing! Your president and general secretary, Reverend W. Wyeth Willard, kindly supplied me with background materials about the Lord's Day League of New England, its predecessor The New England Sabbath Protection League, and The Lord's Day Alliance of the United States. I congratulate you on eighty years of meaningful service as you have sought to carry out your sole purpose which is "to maintain the observance of the Sabbath as a civil rest day, and a day for religious worship."

In some measure next Sunday, March 26, 1983—which is observed as Palm Sunday in Christendom—may be described as "Black Sunday," the day the "Blue Laws" will be repealed in Massachusetts. Then this commonwealth will join with thirty-two states that sanction retail sales on Sunday, leaving Maine as the only New England state where retail stores remain closed on the Lord's Day.

To allow this intrusion on the one day of rest and worship in seven and to seek to justify store openings, as one newspaper has done by warping an adage of faith to say, "The family that shops together stays together" (*Boston Globe*, Monday, March 21, 1983), is to add to the rapid secularization of our day and to move yet further away from the Bible-based moral and ethical precepts on which our country was founded. Our personal and family lives in this state and indeed throughout our nation are the poorer and face even greater challenges as "Black Sunday" approaches!

It is perhaps significant that in the biblical account of Christ's triumphal entry into Jerusalem, as the crowds spread their garments and palm branches before Him, Luke records, "As he approached Jerusalem and saw the city, he wept over it and said, 'If you, even you, had only known on this day what would bring you peace—but now it is hidden from your eyes.' "

Then Christ entered the Temple area and began driving out those who were selling. " 'It is written,' he said to them, 'My house will be a house of prayer, but you have made it a den of robbers' " (Luke 19:41, 45-46, NIV).

Perchance Christ weeps over the cities of Massachusetts today!

But, religious objections aside, it is of note that many Massachusetts merchants oppose Sunday openings and even plead for their customers to continue to shop in stores that will remain closed on Sundays despite the repeal of the "Blue Laws." In last night's *Patriot Ledger,* for example, a local discount department store known both for its bargain merchandise and profitable merchandising methods took its case to the public.

In the ad, arguments against Sunday openings were worded almost in pleading terms on the basis that: 1) The public will not be well served by the extra hours; they are not needed; 2) higher prices will inevitably result from Sunday openings; 3) employees and their families will suffer and be unable to enjoy Sundays as family time in "traditional ways" (including, of course worship services). 4) Note that the "Bargain Center" retained its option of deciding to open Sundays if competition forces them to do so by twice suggesting that this decision to stay closed on Sunday is "for now" or "for the time being."

It is sad that Massachusetts now joins in a movement that will bring higher prices to the public, serve to undermine family life and the worship and leisure time of employees, and force many business people into decisions that are against their better judgment. For this store and many others of principle, the very free enterprise system of our land is jeopardized by the repeal of the so-called "Blue Laws"!

I have entitled these remarks "Is the Battle Lost? Or Some Thoughts on the Internalization of Principle." The Lord's Day League of New England has demonstrated both the knowledge and the tenacity to continue the battle to keep the Lord's Day a day of civil rest and worship. I want you to think with me about another aspect of the battle—one which I believe must be fought and one which can be won.

"In the last days, perilous times shall come" (2 Tim. 3:1*a*) wrote the apostle Paul to Timothy. He continued, in Phillips' translation:

> Men will become utterly self-centered, greedy for money, full of big words. They will be proud and abusive, without any regard for what their parents taught them. They will be utterly lacking in gratitude, reverence and normal human affections. They will be remorseless scandal-mongers, uncontrolled and violent and haters of all that is good. They will be treacherous, reckless and arrogant, loving what gives them pleasure instead of loving God. They will maintain a facade of "religion" but their life denies its truth. . . . From their number come those creatures who . . . are always anxious to learn and yet never able to grasp the truth (2 Tim. 3:1-7, Phillips).

It is probable that we and our children shall live in an increasingly secularized society for many years to come. Despite the best efforts of highly esteemed organizations such as the Lord's Day League, the move of society in the United States, and throughout much of the world, is away from the value system and moral and ethical standards of the Judeo-Christian tradition. Without in any way wishing to suggest that this organization abandon its efforts to reverse recent legislation which breaks down observance of Sunday—the Lord's Day—as a day of civil rest and religious worship, let me affirm that we have an equal responsibility to work to instill within the people of our land values regarding moral standards and ethical conduct which will enable them to live lives of principle even within a secular society.

In recent days New Bedford and all of Massachusetts has demonstrated shock and outrage over a gang rape in a bar which, according to reports, went on for some two hours with spectators cheering participants on. With profound gratitude for the negative reaction to this episode, I must ask why conditions that led to this outrage—open intoxication and callousness of men—have not been attacked before they exploded into violence.

The front page of last night's paper featured a picture of a public official, hand raised, pleading guilty to having part in the payment of $118,000 in bribes to another public official who, when word of the bribery scheme became public, hanged himself. It is relatively easy to shake our heads in disbelief when such a scandal becomes known, but the real question remains—What might have been done in the lives of those involved that could have prevented these tragic circumstances?

The answer, I believe, lies in a recognition that moral and ethical values must come from within; that in the churches, homes, and schools of our land, principles must be instilled into our young that will serve as guiding fundamentals when in later years they shall face temptation to do wrong. Moral and ethical principles imposed from without will be flaunted and disregarded when in secret and when under pressure; moral and ethical convictions early taught and instilled within the individual will serve as the ballast wheel of the ship does to maintain a right course when the storms of temptation arise.

And here we have touched on the real message of God's Word. In Old Testament times, Moses went up into Mount Sinai, and the God who had delivered His chosen people out of bondage said,

Now therefore, if ye will obey my voice indeed, and keep my covenant, then ye shall be a peculiar treasure unto me above all people; for all the earth is mine: And ye shall be unto me a kingdom of priests, and an holy nation (Ex. 19:5-6).

Thereafter, the Ten Commandments were given, and many laws were imposed upon the people—imposed from without, but not a part of their inner being. And much of the Old Testament portrays the battle of God's chosen ones—a battle between their sinful personal desires and what they knew to be the will of God. But, one day, looking to the coming of Jesus Christ, God made a covenant with His people:

This shall be the covenant that I will make with the house of Israel. After those days saith the Lord, I will put my law in their inward parts, and write it in their hearts, and will be their God, and they shall be my people (Jer. 31:33).

What a promise for God's chosen people! For them the day was to come when God's law no longer would be imposed upon them and thus grudgingly obeyed. Now, through Jesus Christ and His presence in their lives, grudging obedience would be changed to a loving desire to be like Jesus and to follow His precepts willingly, joyfully, and completely.

God's covenant spoken by Jeremiah was fulfilled in Jesus Christ. In John 7:37-39 we read:

On the last and greatest day of the feast Jesus stood and said in a loud voice, "If a man is thirsty let him come to me and drink. Whoever believes in me as the Scripture has said, streams of living water will flow from within him" (NIV).

The message of the Book of God affirms that outward

laws, right though they may be, have true meaning only as through God's power they are adopted inwardly to become a part of the warp and woof of the individual life.

Thus, the message to those of us who are concerned for the work of the Lord's Day League of New England becomes a charge that each of us, while continuing to work for legislation that we believe can be justified both on religious and humanitarian grounds, must not consider the battle lost when legislation is enacted which allows retailing on Sunday. That battle continues, but the greater battle is to present to mankind, living today in the secular world and confused by relativism and situation ethics, the good news that moral and ethical principles which are revealed in God's Word and exemplified by Jesus Christ can through God's power become a part of the inmost being and desire of the individual life.

If indeed it be true that our nation shall continue in its trend toward secularization; if the moral and ethical behavior and attitudes of our fellow persons will continue to decline, we have a message of God's grace to proclaim that can enthrone right principles within a person's life and help him to live straight, to observe the Lord's Day, and seek to be like Jesus. The battle is not lost! Our battle can be won as the determination to live right through God's power within is enthroned within the human heart.

But back to that Christian mother of mine. For years I battled against the principles in which she believed; but today, because of her example and the way she pointed me to Jesus Christ, I find through His power that those principles are a part of me that can joyfully be lived, regardless of the way others may go.

The challenge today for the Lord's Day League, while continuing its legislative concerns, is somehow to set forth right principles in the homes, in the schools, and in the churches of our land in the confidence that, through God's power, inner desires can be changed and exemplary lives lived according to the precepts of Almighty God. May we bend every effort to win the battles set before us!

# 13
# The Lord's Day and Natural Resources

## by Harold Lindsell

The Lord's Day Alliance has been a servant of the church since 1888. As we come together nearly a hundred years later I am troubled and perplexed. I have the feeling we may be talking to ourselves; that neither the world nor the church is listening to what we have to say. This may appear to be a grim prospect, but it is better to face reality than to fool ourselves into thinking all is well. With this in mind, let me clear away a few things so as to better orient ourselves before deciding what courses of action are open to us for the Lord's Day and natural resources.

In the United States today, Sunday observance is virtually dead. There are some places where it may still be kept but these are few. Before long, we may expect Sunday to be completely secularized. The death of sabbath day observance has come about for a number of reasons. The first is world secularization and nowhere is this more true than in the Communist world. For multiplied millions of people who have been dragged into the Communist net any possibility for keeping the Lord's Day has evaporated. This is quite understandable, considering the Communist world and life view, and should not come as a shock to anyone.

A second reason for the decline of sabbath keeping lies deep within the Christian church itself. It has been secularized to a degree not fully appreciated by many of its own people. This process of secularization derives from the changing attitude of so many in the church about the written Word of God. In the earliest days of The Lord's Day Alliance, sabbath keeping was based squarely upon the belief that it is an unbreakable command of God. It is an obligation resting on the bald notion of divine authority. It is God's ordinance, not a human one. Mankind indeed needs it, but God has commanded it.

The advent of theological liberalism has changed all of that. The present-day commitment of so many of the church's theologians has nullified the earlier view that Scripture is authoritative and normative. At a time when even the cardinal salvatory doctrines of the Christian faith have been vitiated, and when syncretism and universalism, plus a commitment to revolution and a move toward a Marxist form of socialism, have gripped areas of Christendom, the idea of a binding sabbath commandment seems anachronistic. Given the presuppositions that undergird these theologies, who would disagree that sabbath observance is nonsense?

In the case of liberal theology the crucial factor has been its repudiation of Scripture as normative. But the slide away from keeping the Lord's Day has not come solely among those in the liberal tradition. Evangelicals who claim to take the Scriptures with utmost seriousness are also among those who no longer support sabbath keeping with any real enthusiasm. Evangelicals have been deeply affected by the times in which they live. The dominant philosophy is hedonism. Taken within the context of evangelical theology which stresses the doctrine of grace and denies that man can be saved by works of any kind, freedom and liberty, which indeed are biblical, have been misconstrued. The whole idea of taboos, of "thou shalt nots," of legalism of any kind, is almost passé. The swing of the pendulum away from nineteenth-century

Pietism, or eighteenth-century Puritanism that has such a bad image in the popular mind, has made license of liberty. Situation ethics, denied in principle by evangelicals, has become part and parcel in their life-style so that what they do does not match up with what they say.

This trend among evangelicals with regard to sabbath keeping is related to the broader spectrum of evangelical life. Once the taboos on movies, alcohol, card playing, dancing, and other activities were lifted, it was not unexpected that the taboo with respect to the sabbath should be discarded, too. This is not to say that sabbath observance fits into the same category with these other pastimes. But evangelically minded people have fallen into the trap of assuming there is a dynamic relationship, so that when these other taboos were lifted the sabbath taboo went along with the others.

What I have said so far lays a foundation for my major point—natural resources in relation to the sabbath. If there is to be any recovery of the sabbath principle in relation to natural resources it must be brought about by a return to a proper understanding and use of the Bible by evangelicals. It will not be brought about by this method for theological liberals unless and until they return to a belief in Scripture as truly authoritative. It will not happen among pagans outside the church unless and until they get converted and understand what obedience to the Commandments of God means. It is unlikely that theological liberals will change markedly. We have no reason to suppose that the whole world will be converted.

Thus we are left with the distinct probability that the number of Christians will shrink relative to the total population. There will not be enough of them numerically to make sabbath observance for the right reasons general for all people. What we need to do is to initiate a

two-pronged assault in a battle to restore the Lord's Day
to its proper place.

The sabbath is God's Day. But Jesus said that mankind
was not made for the sabbath. The sabbath was made for
mankind. This suggests the two prongs of the attack I am
about to suggest: mankind in a right relationship to God;
and mankind in a right relationship to nature. Christians
must learn of this twofold meaning of the sabbath and
come to a place where they practice sabbath observance
and also use their energies as member's of Caesar's kingdom to get secular nations to do the same, albeit for different reasons.

Christians primarily celebrate the Lord's Day because
it belongs to God and in it they can worship Him suitably
and with reverential trust and fear. But the sabbath has
in it more than the religious, or human relationship to
God in worship and commitment. It was and is part of
God's natural revelation for humanity in nature itself.
Persons, converted or unconverted, are part of nature
and need the sabbath as earthy people who in their bodies
are inextricably dependent on water, air, and soil.

It is important, even for Christians, to know that they
are tied to the sabbath because it was made for human
physical well-being. And it is this aspect of the sabbath
that can be used to bring the unredeemed to the place
where they will keep it also, but for different reasons that
may be devoid of the primary function of the sabbath,
which is the worship of God. But the reason Christians
should advance to convince unregenerated people to
keep the sabbath is that they need it, that it will work for
their good, and that their failure to keep it is devastating
and assures them of disaster. In this sense one could argue
that outward sabbath observance for unbelievers may be
a form of preevangelism and could open the door wide to
the propagation of the gospel.

First let me make clear that evangelicals believe both in natural and special revelation. Both bear testimony to God, although in different ways. Nature has something to teach us, and special revelation has given the Christian a tool by which to understand natural revelation. Unregenerate persons in the unfolding understanding of nature have learned some things about the divine operations that have benefited them. One knows that one is inextricably related to nature itself and is part of it. No one can deny the existence of the interrelationship.

The cultural mandate of Genesis tells humanity that we are to harness nature and that our physical well-being depends upon nature to a large extent. This can be illustrated in a number of ways. First, there is the food relationship. Without food, people cannot survive. But there is insufficient food in nature itself without human help to feed the world. Thus we must use land to produce wheat, corn, potatoes, and the like. The land is the gift of God. But land is not unlimited. There is only so much of it. The earth itself can be depleted. We already know of lands that have been exhausted by improper use, sometimes through lack of knowledge and at other times because people have exploited it. The same thing is true about trees, some of which give fruit that we can eat, some of which supply timber that can be used for erecting houses, and some of which can be used for firewood in wintertime.

Second, God has put minerals in the ground for our use. But whereas land can be used indefinitely, minerals cannot. There is only so much gold, so much iron, so much oil, so much potash, so much coal. Once they have been consumed, no more will be available. Right now the most liberal estimates indicate that mankind is rapidly approaching the point where many of the minerals we desperately need will be exhausted. We cannot suppose that

we with our inventive genius will not be able to find
substitutes for some or even all of these minerals. Nor can
we suppose that we may not find other sources of energy
of which we have no present knowledge or at least have
no present way of tapping these sources. A few decades
ago atomic energy was simply a dream. Now it has
become a reality, although a dangerous one. Solar energy
is being used in a small way, but its vast potential cannot
be overlooked.

Third, people are a natural resource. People differ from
minerals in that nature has been profligate with respect
to human reproduction. The staggering fact is that the
population of the world did not reach one billion until
around 1850. Today, 135 years later, the population has
almost *quintupled.* It is conservatively estimated that it
will double again in another twenty-five or thirty years at
the most. It is humanity who has affected nature more
than any other plant, animal, or mineral. None of these
has the power to direct and control the use of the natural
resources that we have. We are the master; natural resources are the servants. At the same time, as master we
can only do as we please within certain limitations.

Nature, apart from humanity, has a way of balancing
itself so that it can continue indefinitely. When one species of life overruns the land, counterbalances begin to
operate to offset the imbalance. If certain forms of animal
life overpopulate the land so that the food supply is exhausted, the animals die of starvation. The strong stay
alive to continue the species. In maintaining a natural
balance some animals prey on other animals who provide
food for those that consume them. This helps to keep the
forces of nature in balance.

It is we who have produced nature's great dislocations.
It is we who are consuming the earth's natural resources
and, in the process of using them, threaten not only all of

nature's boundless gifts but ourselves as well. This has come about through the use of land for both good and bad purposes.

Everybody knows now that tobacco and alcohol are two of humanity's greatest enemies. Yet in order to produce them, vast quantities of land, labor, and minerals are used for hurtful ends. Yet we stubbornly resist every effort to change matters, even though we know we should. Not only do the persons who consume these commodities hurt themselves, they also hurt others. Tobacco smoke is a pollutant that takes a toll on those who do not use it but are subjected to its noxious fumes by inconsiderate people who do. Grains that could help feed starving millions are made into alcoholic beverages whose consumption causes industrial and highway accidents and exacts a physical toll via cirrhosis of the liver and a multitude of physical ills that beset those who use it even moderately.

This brings us now to a consideration of the sabbath principle in relation to the greatest of all crises that man has faced, the energy shortage that has caught up with the world. It is only one part of humanity's interrelatedness to nature. Even the solution of the energy problem would be no guarantee that people can at last avert a final depletion of natural resources or that we can prevent what I have called elsewhere the ultimate suicide of mankind. In the short run, however, we can and ought to do something about the energy problem. And it is tied into the sabbath mandate, whether looked at from the vantage point of devotion to God and obedience to His special revelation or to the Creator through natural revelation and man's interrelatedness to nature itself.

Neither people or machines can continue indefinitely without rest. Studies show that human productive capacities vary, depending on the length of time we labor. We require rest and relaxation from production so that we can recover our natural potential. During World War II it became clear that a seven-day week did not increase production. People actually produced less in seven days over the long haul than they did when working six days and resting one. Part of it was physiological; part of it was psychological; all of it was part of the divine plan for nature which is abrogated at human expense. If we, from our study of nature and ourselves wholly apart from Scriptures, refuse to follow the laws of nature, we are in trouble. And whether we like it or not, God has put the universe together so that when we break the physical laws of God, we always ends up by breaking ourselves. Self-preservation, apart from any considerations of the worship of God and our submission to the Creator, should cause us to obey the laws of nature for our own good.

This is true today in a particular and special way because of the energy crisis. One can easily paint a true picture of the benefits the people of any nation would gain if they obeyed God's natural law of one day of rest in seven. This would involve closing down all businesses, including gasoline stations and restaurants every Lord's Day. Since the five-day workweek is commonplace, there is nothing that we must do that cannot be done in six days. No one needs to buy food, dine at restaurants, or purchase goods only one day in the week. Obviously, there will always be works of mercy and necessity that require sabbath day attention. But they are minimal compared to what is done apart from those two phases of life.

If the people of North America stayed off the highways on Sunday alone, except for church attendance or genuine necessities, the energy crisis would be solved or almost solved. There is nothing to show that people buy fewer goods because they cannot buy on Sunday. If all stores and factories were closed one day, nobody would lose anything since none of their competitors would be open either. There would be an immediate 15 percent saving of fuel, electricity, and the like. People would be able to spend time with their families, rest and relax in a less troubled environment, and allow the air of the great cities to recover from the pollution largely caused by automobile exhaust and factory smoke. I should add that at the height of the last energy crunch, Japan laid down a rule that prohibited the use of gasoline on Sunday and it helped that nation greatly.

It might even be that this kind of a Sunday would give us time to reflect on our relation to nature and, in turn, on our relation to the Author of nature and bring us to a knowledge of God. The busyness of life with a secular Sunday, a frantic search for pleasure, and an uncontrolled, hedonistic life can do us no good.

The one day a week would also reduce to manageable proportions the enlarging energy difficulties that promise disaster down the road if something is not done promptly. In a highly technocratic society, the blessings that have come through the automobile, the airplane, and the thousands of concomitant inventions and discoveries have also been a bane. We cannot destroy these things nor can we turn back the clock. But we can lessen their negative impact and produce a more livable world. I know of no easier way to do this than to return to the principle contained in the proper use of the Lord's Day, wholly apart from any religious implications. It can come about by free choice or it can be legislated. It is highly unlikely that it will be accomplished by voluntary action by the citizenry, generally. Therefore the only way to accomplish these objectives is by force of legislative fiat through the duly elected officials of the people.

One could wish that sabbath closing could be brought about on the best of all bases—the recognition that it is the will of God for all people and that they follow this pattern because they wish to worship Him. But short of that, it is still better that it be accomplished, even though the reason for doing it is secular and only has in mind the general needs of people and the benefits that will accrue to them. It would serve the best interests of all people and further human welfare.

Contemporary culture stands opposed to the Lord's Day on grounds that most true Christians believe in and which brought The Lord's Day Alliance into being. Our faith, however, does commit us to the proposition that we are to love our neighbors as we love ourselves. There could be no better way for us to fulfill the Second Commandment than to press for social legislation that would benefit our neighbors, and by our efforts show that we love them as we love ourselves. This would be one of the highest forms of social action that springs from our confession of Jesus Christ as Lord, marks our concern for our fellowman, and identifies us with common and lost humanity in an area of great need.

The bad news is that if something is not done and, done shortly, the plight of mankind must get worse. The good news is that God has given us wisdom and ability by which the worst of conditions can be bettered and approaching disaster can be ameliorated. Surely we have been sent into the kingdom for such a time as this. Let us do something to show that we see the need, sense the opportunity, and are willing to spend ourselves on behalf of mankind in an hour of desperation.

# 14
# Remembering the Lord's Day

by James N. Griffith

The urgency of what The Lord's Day Alliance does was brought home to me in a vivid way from something I read not long ago.

The students of a small Eastern college, numbering about one thousand, took a poll in which they ranked the Ten Commandments according to their own ideas of relative importance. It was most interesting, and also most disturbing, to note that they gave last place to the Fourth Commandment: "Remember the sabbath day, to keep it holy."

Perhaps this underlines in a vivid way the urgency of what is done by The Lord's Day Alliance.

We must be about the business of doing all that we can to preserve the Lord's Day. There are those along with the students who think that the Fourth Commandment of our Lord which has to do with the observance of the sabbath day is of little importance. But this is not so. All of the commandments of our Lord are important.

It is said that General Robert E. Lee once sent word to General Stonewall Jackson that, if he happened to come near campaign headquarters, Lee would like to see him. Jackson, upon hearing this, at once mounted his horse and rode hard through the night and the next day. Arriving, worn and fatigued, he was ushered into the presence of General Lee.

When told that Jackson had ridden hard most of the night and into the day, Lee said, "But Jackson, I told the courier to say that only if you happened to be coming this way, I would like to see you. There was nothing so urgent as to warrant subjecting yourself to undue strain."

Whereupon Jackson replied, "But, sir, the least request of my general is a command to me."

God's Commandment concerning the observance of the sabbath day may not seem as urgent as some of the others, but it must be looked upon as no less than a law and a Commandment of the living Lord. It is a law which facilitates the effective carrying out of God's will concerning worship, Bible study, training in personal Christian service, and needed rest from the rigors of the week.

Our first and most serious conviction arising out of the careful study of the observance of the Lord's Day is that this law of God is necessary. It is a law which arises out of the necessities of man's physical and moral constitution. People, being such as they are physically and morally, cannot be maintained with soundness in either realm without the proper observance and employment of one day in seven as a day of rest and worship.

Experts who have made surveys declare that the person who begins the first day of the workweek 100 percent normal in strength, loses in percentage of vitality more during the working period of that first twenty-four hours than he is able to recover during the rest period of the same twenty-four hours. So the person begins that second day at a level lower than normal. And each succeeding day lowers the tide of his power below the level at which the first workday was begun. It has been discovered that the seventh day provides just enough rest, in addition to the nights of the preceding six days, to restore a person to normal vitality, so that he may start the new week or cycle of seven days alert in mind, sound in body, confident of spirit, and vigorous in the exercise of all energies needed for the accomplishment of his daily task.

The need for rest is a universal necessity. What a person requires, all nature requires. Those of you who were born in rural areas far from the noises of the city, will no doubt remember the sabbath silence which fell upon the earth on each Lord's Day.

Before moving to the city as a boy of ten, I can recall the sabbath quietness of the beautiful meadow near our home. Sunday was different. There was something in the air—a sense of quiet, rest, and repose. There was a solemn stillness. The very songs of the birds, the chirping of the crickets, the voices of the animals seemed to be attuned to a need for solemn reverence.

No one who has lived in the country and walked in the open fields or by the wayside on a sabbath day, could ever fail to see and observe this significant sabbath silence.

But what of the way the Lord's Day is now observed in America and in our own community? Is it a time of worship, a day of rest and quietness? There was a time when the American Lord's Day was an institution held in great honor among our people. Now the slogan "Business as usual on Sunday" heralds the rapidly spreading practice of violating the sanctity of the Lord's Day.

The same men, who as little boys protected their Sunday clothes by sitting quietly in the shade, now keep their places of business open on Sunday in an effort to "put their competitors in the shade."

Almost gone from the American scene is the God-fearing merchant who feels that the greatest service he can render his patrons is to close his store and go to church on Sunday so that he can be the right kind of person on Monday.

Bad as it may sound, the truth is that for millions of people all over the nation, Sunday is fast becoming just

another day. It doesn't come between them and anything
they wish to do, businesswise or pleasurewise. In fact, as
far as many people are concerned, the only things Sunday
comes between are Saturday and Monday.

Once we had a holy day. Now we have joined in making
of this day a holiday. Once everywhere church bells called
us to worship and their call was not ignored. Now the idea
is not worship or rest so much as business and recreation.

The old, self-made preacher was short on education but
long on understanding. He rose to deliver his sermon and
read his text, Matthew 4:24: "They brought unto [Jesus]
all sick people . . . with divers diseases."

"Now the doctors can examine you and usually cure
your ills," he said, "but there is one disease that only the
Lord can cure. That's the divers' disease. And brothers
and sisters, there's a regular epidemic of the divers' disease among us.

"Some dive under the cover and sleep on Sunday morning instead of coming to church. Many others dive for the
couch and watch TV on Sunday night. Some dive for the
lake and stay all day Sunday. Lots of others dive for the
car and take a trip over the weekend.

"Yes, sir," said the old preacher, "The divers' disease is
widespread and only the Lord can cure it."

Of course we do not want to return to the old puritani-
cal observance of the sabbath day. This was stuffy, artificial, and often more pharisaical than Christian. In my
lifetime, I can remember when all a boy was supposed to
do on Sunday was to sit around in his Sunday clothes and
stay clean. But the question that the Fourth Commandment raises is how precisely Sunday should be spent, if it
is to be religiously used. For the Christian, the Lord's Day
stands for the beginning of things, the new creation, and
there is a far greater joy of deliverance: the first day is the
day of the resurrection. On this day the Lord broke the

bonds of death, and He came forth bringing life and immortality to light.

All the postresurrection appearances of Jesus occurred on this day, according to the records of the Gospels and the Epistles. Upon this day, the Holy Spirit descended. Upon this day, from time immememorial the church has assembled for worship; for joyous testimony from lips and lives, for the singing of hymns, for prayer and the preaching of the Word.

Through the preaching of the Word, this day has become the birthday of millions of souls who have trusted Jesus Christ as Savior. For countless Christians, it has been the day of comfort, instruction, inspiration, and fellowship. It is the day of our hope of immortality.

In years gone by, families gathered in an unbroken circle on the Lord's Day. Each had gone his way during the week, but it was a rule of the home that when the Lord's Day came, the children should be at home.

One by one they came with the stories of their pleasure or their pain. Together at the fireside, they told their experiences and found in the family circle comfort for their pains and the fellowship of joy for their pleasure.

The Lord's Day was a day of fellowship, a day for strengthening family unity, and a day for strengthening ties with one another and with God.

There is an old story told of President William McKinley, who in years gone by spent some of his winter vacations in Thomasville, Georgia. Late on a Saturday night one of his advisers arrived from Washington, D.C., and early Sunday morning was shown into McKinley's room. The man said in an excited tone, "Mr. McKinley, I have come all the way from Washington and have brought papers which have to do with your being a candidate for reelection as president of the United States. I would hope that this morning you would review these papers and approve them so that I can be on my way back to Washington."

President McKinley paused for a second and said, "My good man, if I am to become president of the United States by forgetting that this is the sabbath day, then I shall not be president. According to my plans, I am going to church to worship."

It is no wonder, then, that when this martyred president lay dying he was heard to say: "Asleep in Jesus! blessed sleep, From which no one ever wakes to weep."

As the Bible says, "There remaineth therefore a rest to the people of God [. . . a rest for those in Christ Jesus]" (Heb. 4:9). And one day when the weariness of earth is over, all the weary feet of the children of God will turn home again. We shall sit down with our Heavenly Father and with those who have gone before in the home of our Father's rest.

God grant that we shall always remember to keep the Lord's Day as we keep in our hearts the power and the presence of our Lord and Savior.

# 15
# One Day in Seven

### by Robert H. Schuller

One day in seven. Now let's take this Commandment. The sabbath day. The Moslems set a day aside. It's Friday. The Jewish people set a day aside. It is Saturday. Most Christians set a day aside. It is the first day of the week, to commemorate the resurrection of Jesus Christ. You need one day in seven. It is not an ordinary day if you know how to use it. I'll share with you how to use it, because Americans have given it up for the most part.

Traditionally, Sunday was a very great creative day of quietness for faith, for fun, for the family, for the church, and for the community. Something happened—and I make this statement here and now based on research that I have done—and that is, in the past fifty years we have seen a growing, deepening sense of depression in the widespread epidemic of emotional ailments such as anxiety and stress, with its effect upon the human organism. This emotional epidemic of negative, mental, and spiritual problems in our country has risen sharply in proportion to our forsaking of that one day in seven as a useful day for healing.

How can you use it? It's not an ordinary day if you know how to use it. Use it as a day of rest. You need one day in seven to rest the heart, the system, and the body. The Bible says, "In quietness and in confidence shall be your strength" (Isa. 30:15). I try to work hard but I take Mondays off. My sabbath, as you might expect, is not Sunday, and it's not the Jewish Saturday, and it's not the Moslem Friday. My sabbath is Monday. I do not go into my office on that day, because if I can't get my work done in six days, I'm disorganized. Simple. And I would rather live longer and do more than try to accomplish a lot in a few years and die too young. We need one day. Use it for rest. And then use it for a day of retreat. Retreat from the tension-producing inputs that you have to be exposed to the rest of the week.

I'm eternally, profoundly indebted to Richard Neutra for the doctrine of biorealism. I never learned it in theology. But it's embedded in psychology and profound theology. His doctrine of biorealism is that the human being is created with a built-in tranquilizing system, with eyes to see the trees and the hills and colors of the flowers; ears to hear the singing of the birds and listen to the rustle of the leaves and the whisper of the wind; the nose to smell the fragrance of the flowers and the new-mown grass; the skin to feel the caress of the sun and cool breezes. It's a biological reality, and the biological reality is that God created this in order for these to be channels of tranquillity entering your system.

And so when God created Adam, He put him in a beautiful, lush, green garden filled with the exotic fragrance of wild flowers and the melody of singing birds, not in an ugly parking lot where his senses would be assaulted by the wailing of sirens and the exhaust fumes from cars and buses. And that's why when you are in the mountains, you feel the closeness with God. Of course, the bird was designed to fly, the fish was meant to swim, and you were designed to live in a garden. You were not designed to live in a concrete jungle.

So Richard Neutra said, "What can we do? We can't demolish our cities and bulldoze all the asphalt. We need

the cars and we need the buses. What can we do? We have
to design for emotional survival." You bet! So we design
places where you can hear the birds sing, where you can
look out and see the clouds drifting through the sky. And
we try to create a garden retreat from the tension-producing sounds and sights of the world. That's why we need
one day in seven. Now many of you live in cities. You don't
live in a house. You don't live in a place where you're
protected from those sights, so what do you do? I've got
news for you. You go to church on Sunday. That's right!
And that's why many churches are designed with stained-
glass windows and solid walls. Because without them
you'd look out on a parking lot with electric power poles.
But in those beautiful retreat places called churches, the
sounds and sights that would fill you with negative emotional tensions are released and the stress goes.

So it is in our family. Let me say something. We have
a great family—I mean my wife and me and our five
children. We have always kept Sunday as a day to rest; as
a day to retreat—to retreat from the normal pressures of
the week. I remember when our oldest daughter, Sheila,
was about four years old, and her neighborhood playmate
came to the house one Sunday asking if Sheila could come
out and play. I wasn't prepared for that, and I said, "No,
not today, but she can play tomorrow and the next day
and every day the rest of the week, but not on Sunday."
I wanted that one day completely different so that she was
exposed to just the family and friends in the church—
retreat. Let it be a day of rest. Let it be a day of retreat.
Let it be a day to regroup. I mean regroup your thinking
and get your act together.*

---

*Used by permission of Fleming H. Revell Company from the book *Be an
Extraordinary Person in an Ordinary World*, edited by Robert A. Schuller.

# 16
# Call It a Delight

by Leonard J. Hofman

It is a delight for me to gather with other Christians who demonstrate their faith with a follow-through that focuses on the Lord's Day. Our common goal and concern binds us together in a community on fire for the cause of the Lord, a community Elton Trueblood rightly called an "incendiary fellowship."

But does it sometimes seem that you are beating a dead horse? This organization was established in 1888, nearly one hundred years ago, in order "to preserve the Christian Sabbath as a day of rest and worship." But I am sure you will agree that faithful observance of the Lord's Day had been going downhill before that time and has ever since. So I ask, is it worthwhile? Is there a possibility for survival? Is it a dead issue? Will your efforts make a difference?

In response to my own inquiry I submit that the answer is yes, it is worth it, because it is the Lord's Day. Ask me whether any other special day or holiday will continue forever, and I will say no. Either they will be fulfilled with the return and reign of Christ or they will fall by the way when calendars are discontinued. But one day will ultimately come to its own, to blessed fulfillment in Christ's heavenly kingdom. And furthermore, our attitude toward the day here and now will determine whether or not we will enjoy the day there and then.

Let us direct our thoughts toward the Lord's Day of yesterday, today, tomorrow, and forever.

When one turns to the Bible, to those early chapters which record the creation account, one discovers that the Lord God established the day of rest and worship at the beginning. In Genesis 2:2-3 we read,

> By the seventh day God had finished the work he had been doing; so on the seventh day he rested from all his work. And God blessed the seventh day and made it holy, because on it he rested from all the work of creating that he had done (NIV).

And along with the day of rest He established a basic principle of worship before work. We tend to separate work from worship, but God put them together, as though He said: in order to work you must worship, for the person who does not want to worship is not fit for work. After mankind was created the crown of creation, persons were to first spend a day of worship, and then go about working for the Lord. And when the Son of God finished the work of redemption and His body was laid in a grave, He arose on the first day of the week, the Lord's Day.

One can easily trace the sabbath through the Old Testament. In doing so we would see a pattern of instruction and forgetfulness. Upon obedience there was blessing and to disobedience was added warning. The command was clear to celebrate deliverance on the Lord's Day. The Fourth Commandment spells it out boldly, but the familiar path of people was one of forgetfulness and sin. The prophets called to the people of Israel repeatedly promising that the Lord's Day and His blessings go together.

Nowhere is this stated more clearly, and in a style that fits our day, I must say, than in Isaiah 58:13,

> If you keep your feet from breaking the Sabbath and from doing as you please on my holy day, if you call the Sabbath

a delight and the Lord's holy day honorable, and if you honor it by not going your own way and not doing as you please or speaking idle words, then you will find your joy in the Lord, and I will cause you to ride on the heights of the land and to feast on the inheritance of your father Jacob. The mouth of the Lord has spoken (NIV).

It was our Savior who taught us that the Lord's Day was not designed to enslave us. It was a day of freedom and joy. But He did not relinquish His authority when in Mark 2:27-28 He said it was made for mankind, but He retained His lordship over the day.

When we speak of yesterday, we would do well to take note of the teachings of John Calvin who said that the first purpose of the command was to furnish the people of Israel with a type of the spiritual rest, while a second was to assemble on stated days to hear the Word.

The fathers of the Synod of Dordt, 1618-1619, adopted six points, statements which were adopted as well by the Christian Reformed Church already in 1881, not long before the organization of The Lord's Day Alliance. The six points are as follows:

1. There is in the fourth commandment of the divine law a ceremonial and a moral element.
2. The ceremonial element is the rest of the seventh day after creation, and the strict observance of that day imposed especially on the Jewish people.
3. The moral element consists in the fact that a certain definite day is set aside for worship and so much rest as is needful for worship and hallowed meditation.
4. The sabbath of the Jews having been abolished, the day of the Lord must be solemnly hallowed by Christians.
5. Since the times of the apostles this day has always been observed by the ancient church.
6. This day must be so consecrated to worship that on that day we rest from all servile works, except those

which charity and present necessity require; and also
from all such recreations as interfere with worship.

These statements were endorsed anew in 1926. In 1940
the synod of the Christian Reformed Church warned
against work performed by church office-bearers on the
Lord's Day, work "which neither the service of God,
necessity, or mercy required."

As recently as 1974, the synod of the Christian Reformed Church, in keeping with the special resolution as
expressed by the Reformed Ecumenical Synod of 1972,
urged our churches to "guard the celebration of the glad
day of the Lord against the onslaught of secularism" (Acts
of Synod 1974, p. 32).

I was reared in that kind of home. Born into a large
family to humble Christian parents with little formal education, I knew the Lord's Day was a day set apart. The
activities were different, and the rules were strictly applied. More than anything, I remember the day in my
youth as a day of expectancy, when rest and worship were
a part of the atmosphere we breathed. We caught it, we
absorbed it. We never questioned whether worship would
be a part of the day's activities—twice it was expected. We
expected it of our parents and they expected it of us. And
we learned the Heidelberg Catechism which taught us to
answer this question: What is God's will for us in the
Fourth Commandment? And the answer:

First,
    that the gospel ministry and education for it be main-
    tained,
    and that, especially on the festive day of rest,
    I regularly attend the assembly of God's people
        to learn what God's Word teaches,
        to participate in the sacraments,
        to pray to God publicly,

and to bring Christian offerings for the poor.
Second,
    that every day of my life
    I rest from my evil ways,
    let the Lord work in me through his Spirit,
    and so begin already in this life
    the eternal Sabbath.

But what of today? In his book *Megatrends,* John
Naisbitt cited some of the major trends which characterize American society today. Noticeably absent is the persistent and relentless trend toward disregard and
desecration of the Lord's Day. How could one begin to
describe it, and where would one stop? It is the exceptional commercial establishment that is closed on Sunday. It
is the exceptional community that insists on it.

It has become a day for real estate agencies to parade
their houses, and a commencement day for both public
and Christian universities. Something must be said of
sports. We are inundated with promotions of Super Bowl
Sunday, the climactic days of golf tournaments, football,
and baseball series. Joy Davidman, the author of *Smoke on
the Mountain,* a book treating the Ten Commandments,
writing of the report of a Martian student anthropologist
who observed life on our planet earth on a summer Sunday morning while hovering in his flying saucer, quotes
him as writing,

Like so many primitive life forms the creatures of the
third planet are sun worshipers. One day in every seven
is set apart for the adoration of their deity, weather permitting. Their rituals vary, and each apparently involves
a special form of dress; but all are conducted in the open
air, and most seem to require the collection of enormous
crowds. Some creatures gather in vast arenas, to watch
strangely garbed priests perform elaborate ceremonies involving a ball (as a solar symbol, of course, is known to

every Martian schoolboy.) Others, no doubt the mystics and solitaries of their religion, prefer to address the ball themselves with long clubs, singly or in groups of two or four, wandering in green fields. Some, stripping themselves almost naked in their ecstasy, go down to the seashore in great throngs and there perform their rites, often hurling themselves into the waves with frenzied cries. (This practice is unmistakably based on the dogma .... that the sun is a sea god born anew each morning from the ocean; the use of large brightly colored balls in these seaside rituals is confirmatory evidence.) After the ceremonial immersion, devotees have been observed to anoint themselves with holy oils and stretch themselves out full length with eyes closed, in order to surrender themselves entirely to silent communion with the deity.

There exists, however, a small sect of recalcitrants or heretics that does not practice sun worship. These may be identified by their habit of clothing themselves more soberly and completely than the sun worshipers. They too gather in groups, but only to hide from the sun in certain buildings of doubtful use, usually with windows of glass colored to keep out the light. It is not clear whether these creatures are simply unbelievers or whether they are excommunicated from sun worship for some offense—we have not been able to discover what goes on within their buildings, which may perhaps be places of punishment. But it is noteworthy that their faces and gestures show none of the almost orgiastic religious frenzy with which the sun worshippers pursue their devotions. In fact, they usually appear relaxed and even placid, thus indicating minds blank of thought or emotion.

She asked: Was the Martian wrong or right? The day is no longer a holy day, but a holiday. Half the churches are empty while the places of entertainment are crowded. Many persons do not work on Sunday, but how passionately they play.

And what will be the fruit of all this? Have we forgotten that we reap what we sow? Can we really expect a blessing from the Lord on a land that stifles the prayers of its children, that massacres its unborn, that perverts and soils what He creates beautiful and holy, and that disregards His day? He taught us that we reap more of the same.

Many fear tomorrow. We live in fear of a nuclear holocaust, of declining energy supplies, of pollutants. We fear that one day someone may lose control and push a dreaded button. But do we ever think of the fact that people have for generations, and ours the worst, chipped and chiseled away at so foundational an ordinance of God as the Lord's Day? Psalm 11:3 says, "[And] when the foundations are destroyed, what can the righteous do?" (NIV). If our Savior tarries, what will the Lord's Days of tomorrow be?

So much is contingent upon us. But, you say, if it is the Lord's Day and if our track record is so poor, what can we possibly do? Turn to 2 Chronicles 7:14 and read:

> If my people who are called by my name will humble themselves and pray and seek my face and turn from their wicked ways, then I will hear from heaven and forgive their sin and will heal their land (NIV).

Certainly we must do all we can through the means at our disposal as Christian citizens and church members, but first we must radiate to our children, our fellow Christians, our friends, and neighbors, that the Lord's Day is a delight. First they must see that we enjoy the day and know the reasons why. First our churches and spiritual leaders must exhibit their own enthusiasm for a day dedicated to positive spiritual pursuits. First we must return to our King Jesus who is Lord of the day.

If He asks, "How did you observe My day?" would He be pleased to have you reply: I refrained from doing anything? If you add a column of zeros your total is zero. He gave us powerful reasons to celebrate and share. And if Christians do not show leadership in this activity, who will? Our children learn how and why to celebrate the Lord's Day by observing our faith and obedience.

And then one day this emblem of eternal rest will be replaced by reality. The ordinance of paradise lost will characterize life in Paradise regained. The two remnants of perfection, marriage and the Lord's Day, given deeper meaning by Christ's sacrifice and resurrection, will constitute the joy of heaven: a marriage feast and a sabbath rest, Christ and you, in marriage, free, at rest, at last.

# 17
# What I Want to Tell My Students About the Lord's Day

by Clyde Taft McCants

Beyond being moderator of my denomination—which is, after all, a one-year position only—I am also on the faculty at Erskine Theological Seminary, and in and out of my mind over the last several months, the question kept coming to me in that context: What do I want to tell my students about the Lord's Day? What do I want to say to them about their responsibilities and possibilities as pastors in relationship to the Lord's Day?

Part of my background is the pastorate, and I teach now in the department of ministry. I'm concerned specifically with preaching, worship, and the administration of the local congregation. You know, the Lord's Day may just be an important subject for me. And could it also be a subject that we've neglected in the curricula of our theological seminaries? Just what do I have to say to my students about the Lord's Day and how it relates to their ministry?

Perhaps the first thing I'd want to say to them is this: Take the Lord's Day seriously. Make it a serious concern for your teaching and preaching in the church. Enable the members of the congregation to make decisions about this day. Now, let me hasten to say that I'm not suggesting to our future pastors that they bombard their congregations with twenty-five rules on how to keep the sabbath day. Twenty-five wouldn't cover the subject in any case— and that, I take it, is one of the things the Pharisees of

Jesus' day had discovered. I'm not certain that a pastor has any rules on the subject for the congregation outside of what the Scriptures clearly teach when properly interpreted for the life of a post-Easter Christian.

If we try to make rules, they often end up merely being absurd. You may have heard the story of the Mexican woman, Senora Juana Venegas, who came one Sunday morning and handed over to the officials of the church 500 pesos to be used for the building fund. The officers thanked her for what she'd one, but Senora Venegas answered, "No! I didn't do it. My hens did it. The hens layed eggs on the Lord's Day, and somehow it didn't seem right to use that money for ordinary purposes. For several months, I've been setting aside those eggs each week and selling them separately. Now here's the money."

Well, we may admire Senora Venegas's sentiment and her gift, but obviously it wouldn't have done any good to rule that chickens not lay eggs on Sunday. In Due West, South Carolina, the little town where I live, they used to say that the local citizens refused to let the roosters crow on Sunday, but I've lived there thirteen years off and on, and I want to assure you that the roosters crow in spite of the rules. I understand, however, that a number of years ago they did manage to silence a train whistle on Sunday, but surely that's an exception to the rules.

No, I'm afraid the regulations just won't do it. They won't keep a hungry fellow from going into a restaurant and buying a meal on Sunday. They won't keep a family about to be stranded as the result of an empty gas tank from stopping at a station and buying some gas, even at the current prices. For that matter, the rules won't keep a preacher with a sore throat from going into a drugstore and purchasing a much-needed box of cough drops on Sunday. I know whereof I speak. All three of these things I did last Sunday.

And rules from the pulpit have a way of sitting comfortably just up on the visible surface of life. It's very much like the preacher I've heard of whose five-year-old son got up early one Sunday morning and was playing noisily with his new red wagon on the front walk of the manse. When his father heard him, he came out and sent the child scurrying with his wagon to the back of the house—apparently on the grounds that it was the Lord's Day only in the front yard, not in the back.

The rules won't do it. Principles yes, certainly we need principles. I'm certain we need laws, too, laws that sensibly and effectively protect that day of rest each week. But rules for the sabbath lives of individual Christians? No, I'm afraid not. That's definitely not what I'm going to suggest to my students.

What I want them to do, instead, is to take the Lord's Day seriously, to make it a vital part of what they teach and what they preach, to encourage their members to hear and receive God's word to the Christian community about the Lord's Day.

I suspect that we really haven't done that for a long time, that we really haven't made the Lord's Day as vital and significant a subject for teaching and preaching as many of the hundreds of other subjects we address. A few years ago a group of one thousand Massachusetts students were asked to rank the Ten Commandments in their order of importance. Now, you and I may have some questions about ranking God's laws, but the significant point is that the majority of the students placed the Fourth Commandment last, least important of all. I'd like to suggest that the results would be different if ministers were truly taking seriously their responsibility to preach and teach on that Commandment.

I often felt when I began my pastoral ministry that, week after week, my sermons weren't making much impression and that the people weren't interested and stimulated to respond. Then one Sunday I preached on the Fourth Commandment and suddenly I was besieged with comments, discussion, debate, argument, even a compliment or two. What I found out is that beneath the surface people were interested and concerned with this subject. They wanted their pastor to deal with the Lord's Day seriously and responsibly.

Finally, the subject generated enough interest to justify an invitation to one of the state legislators to speak at a family night supper. At that time, the whole subject of the so-called "blue laws" was excessively complicated in my state. As I understood them—and I made a visit to a local law school to find out what I could—the laws made it legal to buy a cooked steak on Sunday but not a raw one; legal to purchase a can of beer, but not a bottle of milk; an ashtray with a picture of a local tourist spot, but not one made of clear glass without the picture. (Granted, I may have misunderstood some of the technicalities, but at least to one reader, the laws were a triumph of confusion.)

One of the things our speaker said that night was that the church needed to straighten out its own act about the Lord's Day and try to make it work among ourselves. In one real sense he was right. Until we really take the Lord's Day seriously with our own people, teach and preach about it, help our congregation wrestle with the issues, and then make responsible decisions, perhaps we don't have a very strong, effective voice in those halls where legislative decisions are made.

That's surely one of the things I want to say to my students preparing for Christian ministry: Take Sunday seriously. Make the Lord's Day a serious concern in your teaching and preaching.

Another point I'd like to share with my students—perhaps it grows out of my own interest in Christian worship, but I honestly believe it goes deeper than that. I want to say to my seminary students and to all pastors that when we restore to Christian worship the sense of joy, excitement, and celebration that it was born with, when we plan for worship and work for it, when we lead it in such a way that it becomes the most important event in the whole week, then our problems with the church people who let the Lord's Day slip by almost unnoticed will begin to draw to an end.

Vital, meaningful Christian worship is irresistible for committed Christian people, and if pastors are willing to work and use the strength and abilities God gives us, we can help worship to be just that kind of experience. I believe that there's no debating that point: the finest, best, most meaningful thing a minister can do to ensure that the Lord's Day truly will be kept by the people of the congregation is to lead in the finest, the best, the most meaningful worship he or she possibly can.

A few weeks ago, I was reading in Willy Rodorf's challenging, sometimes cantankerous book, *Sunday,* and I came across this statement: "If we do not celebrate any Lord's Supper on Sunday we have basically no right to call Sunday the 'Lord's Day.' . . . for the very thing which should make it the Lord's Day, namely the Lord's Supper, is lacking." Far be it from me to debate the issue about when and how often we should celebrate Holy Communion in our churches. John Calvin tried that debate in Geneva with decidely limited success.

I certainly have no intention of advocating the weekly observance of the Lord's Supper to those of you gathered here today. I believe we'll all admit, however, that for all of us, whatever our differing traditions, Communion Sunday is a special time of worship, a time when we are drawn more deeply into the joy and meaning of worship and a time when—whatever our theological explanation of the fact—we feel and know ourselves to be in the presence of our living Lord.

Now, if all worship can be truly joyful and meaningful, as truly special, as those times when we celebrate Holy Communion, then we'll begin to honor the Lord's Day more fully in our churches. If those of us who plan for and *practice* for (I chose that word carefully because I believe earnestly that conducting worship effectively requires *practice*), if those of us who lead in worship will work with God to make worship every Sunday as meaningful, rich, joyful, and special as worship is on Communion Sunday, then many of the difficulties our people have in truly keeping the Lord's Day will begin to disappear.

Samuel Taylor Coleridge, the great British poet, once said, "I feel as if God had, by giving the Sabbath, given fifty-two springs of every year." I say "Amen!" to that, provided those of us who have the opportunity to lead in worship each Sunday are committed to the importance of worship and are willing to make worship as exciting and filled with the Spirit of Christian joy and celebration as we possibly can.

I want my students to hear that word, too, and I pray that I can help to lead them in that kind of worship.

You know, we've all read of "Blue Monday," and we may even have experienced a few. But what is it that makes for a Blue Monday? Isn't it a weekend in which there was just a Sunday and perhaps just a Sunday service —but not a true Lord's Day? Worship that really is special is what makes plain old Sunday into the Lord's Day!

# 18
# The Heritage of the Sabbath

*Exodus 20: 1 Kings 21: 3*

### by Galbraith Hall Todd

We hear much about the preservation of our heritage and rightly so. I ask you to consider the Lord's Day as our heritage as Christians and as a predominantly Christian nation.

## Created in the Beginning

The Lord's Day or sabbath is a heritage coeval with the creation.

> On the seventh day God ended his work which he had made; and he rested on the seventh day from all the work which he had made. And God blessed the seventh day, and sanctified it: because that in it he had rested from all his work which God created and made (Gen. 2:2-3).

In the Hebrew language the word *sabbath* denotes rest.

In Daniel Defoe's great novel, Robinson Crusoe, shipwrecked on a desert island, set up a pole on which he cut notches to mark the days. He made a longer notch for the sabbath day that he might distinguish it from the other working days of the week.

Only two institutions survived the fall of mankind in the Garden of Eden: marriage and the sabbath.

In the ancient Babylonian calendar it was unlawful on the seventh, fourteenth, twenty-first, and twenty-eighth days to do any work.

"The Sabbath was" as the Lord Jesus said, "made for
man." It is written into the constitution of the universe.
As an alternation in the rhythm of life, it is a profound
psychological necessity. Dr. G. Stanley Hall of Clark University, Worcester, Massachusetts, the eminent psycholo-
gist, had studied for the ministry at Union Seminary in
New York, preached at one time for a short period in
Coudersport, Pennsylvania, and in his later years in
Worcester, Massachusetts. He said that the sabbath is so
essential to the welfare of mankind that if religion had not
given us the day, civilization would have been compelled
to invent one.

Following the French Revolution the observance of
Sunday was abrogated. No longer was there to be a day
of rest and worship. In the fourteen months that ensued,
there were twenty thousand more divorces and the in-
sane asylums became overpopulated. As a consequence,
there was a return to the observance of the traditional
day. The Lord God gave us the law of the sabbath as surely
as He ordained the laws of gravity and the harvest in the
realm of nature. At the creation, He set us the example by
His resting at the conclusion of His work. Luther, Calvin,
and the other Reformers taught that the sabbath was instituted for the entire human race.

Henry George called Moses the first great labor leader
and the sabbath his principal reform. It was the labor
leader of another generation, Samuel Gompers, of Jewish
background, who pointed out the fact that seven-day
workers are positively poor workers, lacking the rigor,
stamina, and character so essential to the maintenance of
a sterling personhood. During World War I, Josephus
Daniels, a member of President Wilson's cabinet, said that
the world has learned even in war that sabbath observance is not only a Christian duty but also an industrial
necessity.

In the eloquent words of that peerless orator of the early nineteenth century, Daniel Webster:

> You might as well put out the sun and think to lighten the world with tapers, destroy the attraction of gravity and think to wield the world by human powers as to extinguish the moral illumination of the Sabbath and break the glorious mainspring of the moral government of God.

Luther observed that from the beginning of the world God set apart a sabbath for divine worship. It is a day to remind mankind of God the Creator and Sustainer of life, to prompt us to give due consideration to God's sovereign claim on our time; to call us to the worship of Him, who from the beginning manifested in the sabbath his love, grace, and mercy for humanity. We should mark the fact that it is to be a sabbath to the Lord our God.

Emerson called the sabbath the core of civilization devoted to thought and reverence. In *The Spectator,* Joseph Addison said that if the sabbath were only a human institution it is the best method for polishing and civilizing of mankind. It is a day for us to get our heads out of time and into eternity, out of our finiteness into the infinities which pertain to us who were fashioned to think God's thoughts after Him. The Lord's Day, originally known as the sabbath, is our heritage from the creation.

## Commanded at Sinai

The sabbath is our heritage from Mount Sinai, where the Ten Commandments were given and the nation chosen to be the bearer of the oracles of God had its birth.

The Fourth Commandment enjoining the observance of the sabbath is quite as much a basic moral statute for humanity as the Commandments forbidding murder, theft, adultery, idolatry, slander, covetousness.

Our Savior reverenced the sabbath. Luke's Gospel

states that He went into the synagogue on the sabbath "as his custom was" (4:16).

In Israel the day was not to be one of somberness and gloom. Isaiah said: "[Thou shalt] call the sabbath a delight" (58:13). This spirit of joyousness on the sabbath carried over into the New Testament era and the years that followed. In the extrabiblical Epistle of Barnabas there is the comment: "Wherefore also we keep this day with gladness." The regard for the day as one of joy is epitomized in the declaration of the psalmist: "This is the day which the Lord hath made. We will rejoice and be glad in it" (Ps. 118:24). Christopher Wordsworth in his familiar hymn celebrates the sabbath as: "O day of rest and gladness, O day of joy and light." The day was intended to bring happiness to the family, and relief to the household servants from accustomed duties, to the stranger within the gates, and even to the beasts of burden.

I wonder how many of you are familiar with the writings of Dr. Edward A. Steiner of Grinnel College in Iowa, a Congregational minister, who was converted from Judaism. Dr. Steiner, well-known author on the Americanization of immigrants, depicted the sabbaths of his early years in a Jewish ghetto of his ancestral land as a quiet, happy day in the family and the home following attendance at the synagogue.

In an old, quite remarkable book on the sabbath by James Gilfillan, a minister in Stirling, Scotland, the author asked the question:

> What Sabbath observing nation, it has been asked, has ever been barbarous or ignorant? The lands of the Sabbath and the Bible have always been the chosen abode of knowledge and the lights of the earth.

On a tablet on the facade of the Allegheny County courthouse in Pittsburgh, the work of the renowned architect H. H. Richardson, there is a tablet inscribed with the Ten Commandments. That great tablet, designed so that one who runs may read, is a governmental recognition of the Decalogue as the fundamental law of well-ordered society. The sabbath is an integral part of that moral code.

The sabbath is our heritage from Mount Sinai and God's ancient people Israel.

## Renewed at the Resurrection

The Lord's Day or Christian sabbath is our heritage from the resurrection of Jesus Christ and the earliest days of the Christian church.

Our Savior, after resting in the tomb following the completion of His atoning work on the cross on the final sabbath of the old covenant, rose from the dead on the first day of the week. Henceforth, Christians transferred their sabbath to the first day of the week. It was on that day, the Day of Pentecost, that the Holy Spirit descended to empower the church. The first person to record for all time the term "the Lord's Day" was the beloved disciple John, who testified: "I was in the Spirit on the Lord's Day" (Rev. 1:10).

In AD 321, four years prior to the Council of Nicea, the Emperor Constantine issued the decree that all judges with the civil population, together with those engaged in the workshops of artisans should rest upon the venerable day of the sun.

John Eliot, who first translated the Scriptures into an American Indian language, held that our whole religion fares according to our sabbath observance. Poorly observed sabbaths make poor Christians.

Louise Randall Pierson in her book *Roughly Speaking* told how, during the depression era to finance the education of her children, she had opened a roadhouse in New

England. At the height of the Sunday dinner hour, the local constable appeared, saying: "You are under arrest. This is the Lord's Day."

She commented: "I had lived in New York state so long that I did not know the Lord had a day." That would be true of many of our states today.

We must remember that Sunday is the Lord's Day—no one else's. Voltaire is said to have averred that if you would destroy Christianity you must first kill Sunday.

The Lord's Day is our heritage from the resurrection of Jesus Christ and the first disciples of our Lord.

### Our American Heritage

The Lord's Day is our heritage from the founding fathers of our nation.

The Pilgrims left England where King James decreed that Sunday should be a day of sports and amusements. They approached the shores of Cape Cod on a Saturday in December, 1620. Not desiring to land on the Lord's Day, they tarried on Clark's Island and spent a day of sabbatic rest and worship. In many respects, Clark's Island is as significant as Plymouth Rock.

Preaching at a national sabbath convention at Saratoga, New York, in 1863, Mark Hopkins, the physician who became a minister, philosopher, and the famous president of Williams College, said:

> History shows that God has joined freedom with the Sabbath, with English and American liberty. The Sabbath Day was the turning point. Freedom has always found the best name and truest defenders in those parts of the country where the Sabbath has been most honored. The civil as based on the religious Sabbath is an institution to which society has a natural right precisely as it has to property.

Lord Byron in *Childe Harold's Pilgrimage* described a

Sunday in Spain, which must have contrasted sharply with the sabbath days he had known in Aberdeen. In Spain, it was the day of the bullfight.

> The Sabbath comes, a day of
>     blessed rest;
> What hallows it upon this
>     Christian shore?
> Lo, it is sacred to a solemn feast;
> Hark! heard you not the
>     forest-monarch's roar?

He portrayed the scene further:

> Yells the mad crowd over
>     entrails freshly torn,
> Nor shrinks the female eye,
>     nor e'en affects to mourn.
>
> .................................................................
> Such the ungentle sport that
>     oft invites
> The Spanish maid,
>     and cheers the Spanish swain;
> Nurtured in blood betimes,
>     his heart delights
> In vengeance, gloating
>     on another's pain.
> What private feuds the
>     troubled village stain!

On one occasion, Orville Wright of Dayton, Ohio, was invited by King Alphonso of Spain to present an airplane exhibition on Sunday. Notwithstanding the fact it was a command performance, Mr. Wright declined to hold it on Sunday. His religious convictions on the matter were derived, no doubt, from his upbringing in the home of his father, Bishop Milton Wright of the United Brethren Church.

I fear that our own nation is drifting rapidly into a state where the Lord's Day is both desecrated and quite ignored. It is a legacy which we must safeguard and cherish. The Dutch called the day God's Dyke, a bulwark against the insidious inroads of secularism, materialism, and paganism. The laws of at least forty-seven of our states once had statutes which would constitute barriers to protect the people from those who would rob them of the Lord's Day.

We need to inform the enemies of the Lord's Day in the courageous language of Naboth addressed to the wicked King Ahab: "The Lord forbid it me, that I should give the inheritance of my fathers unto thee" (2 Kings 21:3).

In the words of the great Princeton theologian, Dr. Benjamin Breckinridge Warfield: "The Lord's Day (the Christian Sabbath) is placed in our hands by the authority of the apostles of Christ, under the undiminished sanction of the eternal law of God."

# 19

# How Providence Made a Believer of a Doubting Thomas

by Hugh Cates

"Do real Christians have real doubts?"

As I looked around the room that February day, I wondered how many of the Christians gathered at the table shared my nonverbalized thought as to whether or not what we had just decided to do was possible.

As acting chairman of the communications committee, my job was to propose a course of action to be followed during the coming year. This was not an easy task, as I had only been a part of this ninety-year-old volunteer, inter-denominational organization for less than six months and this was my very first committee meeting.

A wiser member of the small group had suggested we narrow our sights to just three undertakings, instead of trying to tackle the myriad of projects discussed. "Let's not scatter our shots," he had said, studying the faces of his fellow committee members, "but let's just 'zero-in' on these three."

John Nix, a lawyer, had been a member of the board for seven years. The half dozen or so men and one woman present had quickly agreed this was the best course of action.

Talk centered on the most exotic of the three proposals: the production of thirty-minute, full-color, sound motion picture about preserving the sanctity of Sunday. No one present had ever produced a movie, but this did not lessen the enthusiasm of the seven managers and the executive director.

Mine was a case of mixed emotions. While caught up in the excitement of the moment, I had serious doubts. I had been in the print-related public relations field for almost thirty years and was a realist enough to know that films just don't happen. I was somewhat familiar with the problems confronting the group. Or, at least, I thought I knew what to expect in the way of obstacles—not the least of which was lack of money.

But Providence was about to intervene, the first of many times this was to happen.

"Hugh, how much money is needed to produce a thirty-minute film?" The quiet feminine voice articulated the question on the minds of the others. This was her first meeting, since being appointed to take the seat of her husband, the owner of a motel chain, who had died of cancer just two months before.

"Roughly $40,000," I answered.

The murmuring indicated amazement at the high costs of making a film.

It seemed no one, the chairman included, remembered the Christian's definition of faith: " . . . the substance of things hoped for, the evidence of things not seen" (Heb. 11:1).

"I think," she said, in a deliberate tone, "I know where I can get $20,000.

A hush fell over the group.

Then pandemonium broke loose as everyone tried to talk at once.

"Deen, that's great," I said. It seemed too good to be true. None appeared to be aware that Providence had become a part of the venture.

"A half of a movie is better than no movie at all," someone observed, after a quick calculation. All heartily agreed.

Knowing the limitations of programing, I said, "If we wish free public service time on TV, we still have a problem. Scheduling is done in half-hour increments and a fifteen-minute film will simply not be acceptable by a station." While the film was to be shown in churches and at other places, we were counting heavily on showing it on television, too.

Evidently, my faith was not complete. Why was I not encouraged instead of discouraged? The obvious monetary deficit seemed to be insurmountable.

*Old doubting Thomas,* I thought to myself as I strove hard to deal with my own misgivings.

"Why don't we proceed with plans for a fifteen-minute film and perhaps God will show us the way?" Again John Nix came to the rescue. Little did the Christian lawyer realize then how God was to deal with this specific problem, but only *after* the shorter version of the film had been shot and edited.

Trying not to let my feelings show, I thought of a quotation by Elton Trueblood, "Deliberate mediocrity is a heresy and a sin. To make your life small when it could be large is a sin of the worst kind." I knew his saying was somehow applicable to my doubting-Thomas mind-set and I thought of the inertia which generally follows such thinking. "John, this is the only way we can proceed," I said.

The meeting moved at a brisk pace after John's suggestion. Everyone was exhilarated. It was quickly decided that four concepts were to be included in the script: worship, rest, family fellowship, and service to others.

So many wonderful things happened during the filming that the committee automatically accepted the occurrences as only an answer to prayer through the Providence of God. One manager, Dr. Franklin Sellers of Chicago, wrote me sometime after the meeting with the perfect solution for placing a fifteen-minute movie in a thirty-minute time slot. The answer was so obvious it was apparently difficult, at first, to see: Have a three-member panel critique the four concepts immediately following the telecasting of the film. This we were later to do.

Many of the committee members were present at the film's first screening. At the movie's end, a lump began to swell in my throat as the simple tag line, which the executive director of The Lord's Day Alliance and I had privately decided upon, appeared on the screen: "In memory of Cecil B. Day, Sr."

I quickly glanced across the dimly lit room at John and at the lone, thoroughly surprised committeewoman, the one who had first made me aware during work on this project of the providential hand of God.

For some unknown reason, my thoughts turned briefly to what Benjamin Franklin had once said, "God was no idle spectator when this nation of ours was formed." I'm firmly convinced that God was part of this small enterprise, since it *was* within the framework of His will.

I thought to myself, *To all those who helped with the film, I'm truly indebted—especially to two persons, in particular.*

I continued staring at these two new friends, as I silently thanked the Almighty for both of them, John, the wise counselor, and Deen, Mrs. Cecil B. Day, Sr.

### It's Providential . . .

"It's providential" was a phrase oft repeated throughout the filming of *The Lord's Day*.

Here are a few examples of what prompted this statement:

(1)  The film production costs of twenty thousand dollars came almost miraculously from nowhere.

(2)  The content of the film took a one-hundred-eighty-degree turn from that of a Sodom-and-Gomorrah, hell-fire mind-set to that of a positive motivational movie.

(3)  The selection of a cinematographer/director occurred after much prayer and multiple recommendations of the person finally selected.

(4)  Through the cinematographer a scriptwriter was selected who, it turned out, at one time had studied for the ministry. For four years, this person had written motivational material for Earl Nightengale in Chicago.

(5)  Through the scriptwriter the narrator, Alexander Scourby, was obtained. Mr. Scourby is tops in his field.

(6)  Nonactor/actress types were selected and they performed almost beyond their ability. Unbeknownst at the time to the person doing the casting, among those selected were a former Miss Georgia and a lady who had taught dramatics at the college level in Louisville, Kentucky, fifty years earlier.

(7)  An old car was needed for a flashback scene and it was suddenly available.

(8)  The church selected as the shooting site had to be relatable to persons of many faiths. The church selected turned out to be within a "stone's throw" of the home of the scriptwriter where this decision was made.

(9)  Less than two months after the selection of the shooting site, the film was reviewed by the members of the board of managers of The Lord's Day

Alliance of the United States at the board's annual meeting in Texas.

(10) Three months later in Georgia, videotaping was done of the film, plus a three-member panel consisting of a former Miss America, the president of the Alliance, and the pastor of the church featured in the movie.

(11) Three months afterwards, the half-hour videotaped program was telecast in what is the sixteenth largest, and perhaps tenth most important, market in the United States, a viewing area which has 1.5 percent of the nation's population.

(12) At this writing, distribution of the film has extended from California to England.

# 20
# The Rest We Need
*Ezekiel 20: 10-22*

### by Andrew R. Bird, Jr.

One of the primary rules for finding lost things is that you first empty your mind of any preconceived ideas.

One of the main causes for failing to find something you are looking for is that you have a certain preconceived idea about what it must look like or where it must be. Let's say your wife sends you to the cupboard to look for a box of soap, but you cannot find it anywhere. Then your wife looks, and she says, "Why here it is, right in plain sight." The reason you failed to find it is that you had always thought that the soap you were looking for came in a red box, and you thought it was on the third shelf from the bottom. So, though you looked everywhere, you were really looking for a red box on the third shelf from the bottom, and the things you saw on the other shelves didn't really make any impression. But your wife found it at once in a blue box on the top shelf, and you would have found it too, if you had taken the trouble to clean the preconceived ideas out of your mind.

This simple rule applies, too, when you look for what is wrong with our world. We must also get rid of preconceived ideas when we look for what is wrong with our lives. So when we start looking around for answers to some of our deepest uncertainties, we also tend to do our looking bound by certain preconceived ideas.

Today, for example, when high taxes keep rocking us

back on our heels and inflation continues its upward spi-
ral, and the general world situation seems to be getting
worse instead of better, we tend to think that the trouble
must lie somewhere in Washington, or Paris, or Jerusalem, or Tehran, or Cairo, or London, or Moscow. The
world's leaders must be the cause of our problems. Our
President must not be doing his job well. Or the prime
minister or the lawmakers must be extremely inefficient.
We are quite sure that many of our own personal problems must somehow be related to the fact that some important people in our world are bungling things up so
badly. Everyone assumes this, and our mass media support this assumption by reporting the great events that
happen on high level. When we look for reasons why so
many things are going wrong in our world, we look only
in certain places and then at only certain people.

Now, it is possible, wouldn't you agree, that the cause
of so much that is wrong with our world and with our lives
is actually to be found elsewhere. Surely, our leaders
make mistakes and our lawmakers and law enforcers can
be disappointing at times. But couldn't it be that they,
along with all of us, are caught up in a bad state of affairs
that is caused by some force or set of circumstances that
none of us have really taken too seriously? Maybe we are
looking in the wrong places and at the wrong people
when we look for the source of the decay and confusion.

But if you are willing to admit that the cause just might
well lie in some unexpected place, and be a quite unexpected matter, there is something I think we should consider. It is found in the Bible, that highly respected but
so-often-ignored book! What is more, it is found in that
part of the Bible we often call the Ten Commandments.
And that is a part of the Bible people have not shown very
much interest in lately. What is more, it is the Fourth
Commandment that provides the clue to what is wrong

with our times. And that makes this thing I want to bring up probably the last thing anyone thinks about when they try to describe what is wrong in our world.

### The Day of Rest

The Fourth Commandment is about the sabbath day. The sabbath day was the seventh day of the week for the Hebrew people—that would be Saturday for us. There are some people within the Christian tradition who still keep the seventh day as their sabbath. But, for the most part, Christians today have made the first day of the week their sabbath—their day of special rest, devoted to God.

This was done already in New Testament times, apparently because Christ rose on Sunday and the Holy Spirit was given on Sunday. Furthermore, the Christian Sunday was from the first a day in which Christians devoted themselves to their Lord. In the Old Testament, already, special gifts were presented to God on the first day of the week as Leviticus 23:11 tells us. Whatever the reason, Sunday has become the holy day of rest for most Christian people and the Fourth Commandment is about this special day.

The Fourth Commandment says:

> Remember the sabbath day to keep it holy. Six days you shall labor and do all your work; but the seventh day is a sabbath to the Lord your God; in it you shall not do any work, you, or your son, or your daughter, your manservant, or your maidservant, or your cattle, or the sojourner who is within your gates; for in six days the Lord made heaven and earth, the sea and all that is in them, and rested the seventh day; therefore, the Lord blessed the sabbath day and hallowed it (Ex. 20:8-11, RSV).

The point of this somewhat obscure language is that God has set aside a special day of rest for His people and requires them to observe it. This day of rest is something like a weekly holiday. On our national holidays, there are certain prescribed patterns of behavior. Regular work is halted and there are parades and various kinds of celebrations. The special day God gave His people was to be a day of holy assembly for worship and for hearing God's Word. The Christian tradition has always recognized that the sabbath must still be a day of public worship and of modified behavior that makes the day different from all the rest.

### No Rest Means Trouble

The person who fails to keep this day of rest will be in trouble, and the nation that consistently desecrates this day of rest will be in trouble, too. In fact, the widespread desecration of this day is one of the reasons we are in such deep and serious trouble right now.

"You cannot be serious?" I can just about hear you say that. It seems too out of place to suggest that one of the main causes of the world's problems is the widespread desecration of God's day of rest.

But look at it this way. This is a Commandment that God has designed to affect all of society. God does not just say, "I want you to rest one day out of seven," but He very explicitly says that He wants this to apply to everybody in your household and to everyone who works for you, and even to your animals. This Commandment is recorded in both the Book of Exodus and the Book of Deuteronomy, and in both cases there is a careful naming of sons, daughters, oxen, asses, and visitors. Everyone must keep the day of rest because everybody needs it.

So you see, the Commandment was designed to affect all of society. That would imply, wouldn't it, that if people disregard it and make Sunday an ordinary day of regular work and hard play, the entire structure of society is bound to suffer?

That is why I say that this is one of the places we should look when we are trying to find out what it is that has caused our society to decay so rapidly during the last days. Who really keeps a day of rest as God wants it kept? Millions of people, many of them claiming to be Christians, have made the Lord's Day a day of "business as usual" and of fun and games. When great numbers of people break the commands of God that way, there are bound to be grave problems in society.

## The Lesson of Israel

But if you still doubt that failure to observe the day of rest God has given causes grave problems in society, the ancient nation of Israel demonstrated that it did in their national life. Even though they were the first to receive God's great Commandment concerning the day of rest, they were often unwilling to stop their work. The prophet Amos recalled their impatience with their sabbath and their eagerness that it be over with so that they could get back to their daily work. As a result, the moral tone of the nation collapsed—and injustice was found everywhere! This is what the Book of Amos says in the eighth chapter:

> Hear this, you who trample upon the needy, and bring the poor of the land to an end, saying, "When will the new moon be over, that we may sell grain? And the sabbath, that we may offer wheat for sale, that we may make the ephah small and the shekel great, and deal deceitfully with false balances, that we may buy the poor for silver and the needy for a pair of sandals, and sell the refuse of the wheat?" (vv. 4-6, RSV).

You see, the people couldn't wait until their religious observances were finished and their day of rest was passed. What happened? The poor were oppressed, and there was cheating and stealing. The prophet Amos continued by announcing the judgment of God upon His sabbath-breaking people.

## A Personal Decision?

Now, you may ask, "Why, though, does the desecration of the sabbath have such a widespread effect?" Whether or not one wants to devote a special day to the Lord is a purely personal decision, isn't it? Isn't it a little absurd to say that the failure of many people to observe the day of rest is the cause of many of the problems in our modern world?

Not really! Whether or not people observe a day of rest depends upon their view of God and of their lives. Why don't people keep the sabbath holy today? They think that they must work and play just as hard as they can and do as they please seven days a week, or else their lives just will not be worthwhile. They don't really trust God. They trust themselves, and they think that their material success depends entirely upon their own hard work and shrewdness.

It takes a certain kind of faith in God to back off from your ordinary work and play when Sunday comes around, to arrange your life so that there will be nothing that will interfere with your worship of God and with your sharing the truth of God with your friends and family. There are so many things that tempt us on Sunday these days. But the person that really trusts God knows that there is nothing more important than worshiping the Lord and keeping His holy day. We should know that, after all, happiness is not secured by hard work and hard play. Our happiness depends on God—first, last, and always. He will take care of us.

This is why those who insist that Sunday is their day to

do with as they please become people who are nervous and desperate when it comes to their own welfare, because they think their welfare depends mainly on their efforts. So then, today, the great nations of the world are in economic difficulty. In many of them, welfare rolls are swelling and there is corruption and crime. When it comes right down to it, we should know better than to put our trust into our own efforts for our own salvation and well-being. We all know that no matter how hard we try, we are not going to be able to escape tragedy and disappointment.

## Jesus Offers Eternal Rest

Today God comes to us in Jesus Christ. Jesus died for human sins. Jesus promises those who believe on Him that He will take care of them throughout this life. "Come to me, all who labor and are heavy laden, and I will give you rest" (Matt. 11:28, RSV).
And Jesus promises eternal life to all those who believe in Him. He said, "For this is the will of my Father, that every one who sees the Son and believes in him should have eternal life; and I will raise him up at the last day" (John 6:40, RSV).

Now that God has revealed Himself in Jesus Christ, it is foolish to go on living as if everything depended upon our efforts. But people keep saying that the day of rest is their day to do as they please. In some cases, churches are willing to reschedule their services so that people can have the entire Sunday to pursue their own pleasures. How about that?!

When most everybody today is desecrating the day of the Lord, and using it for their own selfish purposes, it is no wonder, really, that there is such a breakdown of basic human qualities like love, compassion, and fairness. If you chronically forget to keep the Lord's rest day, it is no wonder, really, that life seems so flat and tasteless and disappointing to you!

If you are looking for the causes of modern decay and degeneracy, don't look just at the world's capitals, at the big places where the big people make big decisions. Look into the law of God. Look at the Fourth Commandment. One of the reasons there is so little tranquillity and peace today is that people have failed to put their trust in God. They trust themselves alone and show it by refusing to keep God's day holy. That is one of the reasons your life is so shaky and disappointing, too. You are living at the same hectic pace seven days a week, desecrating the day of rest God has commanded you to keep!

God comes to you now in the Lord Jesus Christ, His only begotten Son. Don't be so frantic about making a living and having fun. Don't worry about the day of death. Put your trust in Jesus. He will take care of you and make your life significant and your faith a moment of victory! Express your trust in the Lord by making every Sunday a day of rest devoted to your Savior.

The rewards God gives those who honor Him are unimaginably great!

# 21
# Heaven-sent Leisure

*Mark 6:31*

**by H. J. W. Legerton**

The Lord's disciples were full of zeal for His service, so much so that they overlooked their own basic needs. With His ever-loving concern for His dear ones, the Lord Jesus called their attention to this and bade them "Come . . . apart" and "rest a while." Like so many of us today, they led busy lives; there were many "coming and going" with the result that "they had no leisure."

Leisure forms an important part of modern life. A "five-day week" is enjoyed by many and still there is a craving for yet more leisure. Someone has said that if this general trend continues we may soon have a "five-day weekend." So large does the subject figure that a British professor has written a thesis on "The Problem of Leisure." It is one thing to have more and more leisure, and quite another to know how best to use it. It is not my purpose to deal with the general subject, but rather to call attention to the divinely instituted fundamental leisure.

The Creator, having made man and woman, breathed into them the breath of life and then provided for them those things that would meet their bodily, mental, and spiritual needs, needs which still call for attention.

Genesis, chapter 2 verses 1-3, not only record that, following the work of creation, God ceased from that work on the seventh day, but that He blessed and sanctified that day, that is, He appointed the principle of one day's rest out of the seven days of the week. Thus we have the record of the first provision of "leisure," all the more important because of its divine origin. The Seventh Earl of Shaftesbury declared: "The longer I live the more I reverence and adore the benevolent wisdom of God which has set apart one day in seven for his Service and man's refreshment."

Let us look at four main purposes of this heaven-sent leisure.

### Cessation

To cease from everyday labor one day each week is essential for physical well-being and the preservation of health. Dr. Haegler of Basel stated "each day is marked by a gradual failing of the nervous energy of the worker, with a return to normal conditions after the Sunday rest," and he is by no means alone in the medical profession to underline the basic necessity of such rest. The writer Addison put it another way: "Sunday clears away the rust of the whole week." We all know what devastation rust can cause to an automobile unless it is dealt with, so will the human body suffer unless this weekly respite is observed. We ignore this purpose of Sunday leisure at our peril.

### Concentration

The "comings and goings" of modern life all too often mean that, in the rush and noise of the daily round, our focus is limited to material things which, though necessary in time, are of no value for eternity. The apostle John tells us in Revelation 1:10 that he was "in the Spirit on the Lord's Day." He used the first day of the week to concentrate upon spiritual values, which is another of the great purposes for which God gave the sabbath, Matthew Arnold lamented:

What shelter to grow ripe is ours?
What leisure to grow wise?

...................................................................

Too fast we live, too much are tried
Too harass'd to attain
Wordsworth's sweet calm, or Geothe's wide
And luminous view to gain.

Of course what we need is more than Wordsworth or Goethe; we desperately need "the peace of God which passeth all understanding" (Phil. 4:7); hence He says: "Be still, and know that I am God" (Ps. 46:10). Thus one day in seven we have the inestimable benefit of concentrating upon our Savior, the fairest among ten thousand.

### Consecration

We must not overlook the fact that God has commanded that we "Remember the sabbath day, to keep it holy." "Holy" means "set apart," "separated," "Consecrated to God." The day, though given for man's benefit, belongs to God ("the sabbath of the Lord thy God," Ex. 20:10; "the son of Man is Lord also of the sabbath," Mark 2:28) and, as such, should be devoted to His worship and service. Shall we take the gift and ignore the Giver? Shall we use the day for our own purposes and leave out of its hallowed hours the Heavenly Father Who instituted it for His glory?

A Church of England report stated:

In these days of hurry and overstrain no greater boon could be conferred on the community than the recovery of its quiet Sunday to be a day of worship that shall infuse the spirit of Worship into the whole of life and its every activity.

If the first day of every week is consecrated to God, the

days that follow will experience something of that holiness which will make life all the sweeter.

**Consideration**

Speaking to His people Israel concerning the sabbath, God reminded them that this great institution was not only for an individual but also for the family "thy son, ... thy daughter" and for others who serve them "that thy manservant and thy maidservant may rest as well as thou" (Deut. 5:14). One of the prevailing sins of our time is selfishness; "I'm all right, Jack!" "Am I my brother's keeper?" Do we value our Sunday freedom, do we claim the right to do as we like on our free day?

Listen to the apostle Paul on this subject (Gal. 5:13): "ye have been called unto liberty; only use not liberty for an occasion to the flesh, but by love serve one another." There are certain works of necessity and mercy (public services, hospitals, and so forth) that must be performed every day, but do let us abstain from those activities on the Lord's Day which will involve others in unnecessary labor and cause them to lose their Sunday, which they may value quite as much as we do. The sabbath day can be a marvelous antidote to the selfishness to which we are all so prone.

There is much truth in the saying that we never miss anything until we've lost it. If we continue to be careless about the manner in which we spend Sunday and if the day goes on being exploited by commercial interests, we shall wake up one day to find it gone, lost forever, to our own incalculable loss.

Have you ever tried to visualize what it would be like if we had no sabbath, if there were no specific day set apart so that, as families, as communities, we had no break, no respite from noise and bustle, no "shelter to grow ripe, . . . [no] leisure to grow wise," no gathering together in fellowship, no longer able to sing, as did Isaac Watts, "How pleased and blessed was I, to hear the people cry, Come let us seek our God today"? Henry Ward Beecher put it in this telling manner: "A world without a Sabbath would be like a man without a smile, like a summer without flowers, and like a homestead without a garden. It is the joyous day of the whole week."

Despite all the encroachments which have been made upon the sacred ground of the sabbath, all the infiltrations of secularism, we have our lovely inheritance in a measure. Let us then defend, nourish, preserve, and use rightly this precious treasure, and hand it down to our children as we received it from our fathers.

"Come ye yourselves apart and rest awhile."

# 22
# The Christian Lord's Day

by Aaron N. Mekel

During the days of the Second World War, an American serviceman wrote a letter to his loved ones at home. In this letter he told them how he managed to keep the spirit of the Christian sabbath. Here was a boy, thousands of miles from home, quite likely lonely and a bit distraught, yet true to his basic convictions. He told his loved ones how he tried to synchronize his own personal observance of Sunday with theirs. "When I think you are in church," he said, "where I myself would love so much to be, I just open my Bible, read a few verses, and, in the inner temple of my heart, say a prayer for you and the welfare of all men."

That is pretty good, isn't it, for a lad thousands of miles from home, seeking to keep the spirit of the sabbath inviolate? The remembrance of that Christian sabbath in his home held him fast and strong and true. Someone has truly said that Sunday is the core of our civilization—a day dedicated to thought and reverence.

Now let us make it clear that we are not advocating blue-lawism. Not at all. We are not pleading in this chapter for a revival of the kind of sabbath our Lord had to contend with in His day, or even for a return of the Puritan sabbath of early New England.

This is not to say that I do not greatly admire the spirit of those old-timers of the Puritan Commonwealth. We moderns can hardly afford to give "three sneers" for the Puritans! They might have been somewhat somber and forbidding, but, believe me, they had something we need today. They had moral backbone.

I have been reading up on some of the quaint customs of the Puritan sabbath. Imagine sermons three hours long! What in the world would some of you, who have trouble keeping awake twenty or thirty minutes, ever do on that basis! And some of their habits were quaint, to say the least. Did you know, for instance, that they had a tithing man whose duty it was, whenever he saw someone's head nodding, to give them a strong rap on the head with a long pole? Personally, I am glad we have a better use for our deacons today! In Virginia they had a custom of passing around a snuffbox when someone got sleepy. What a cure for boring sermons! Yet with it all, our admiration goes out to those stern souls who laid the keel for our nation.

Then there were the rather weird and strange customs of the Pharisees of Jesus' day. A woman was not allowed to look in a mirror, because if she did she might see a gray hair and try to pull it out, and that would be breaking the sabbath! People were not allowed to wear artificial teeth on the sabbath day. So, as someone has suggested, the saints did not look their prettiest on the sabbath. And so on and on—ad nauseam.

But none of that for our Lord Jesus Christ! He rescued the ancient sabbath from its negative misuse and translated it into a radiant, positive, glad day. So much so that today we have a hymn in which we sing: "O day of rest and gladness, . . . most beautiful, most bright."

Jesus, in fact, transfigured the ancient sabbath through His own victory over death—so that today we keep not the seventh day of the week, but the first, the Christian Lord's Day, as a memorial to His great victory over the "last enemy."

When His contemporaries criticized His hungry disciples for plucking a few ears of grain on the sabbath, Jesus held them at bay. When they criticized Him for healing the sick, He replied, "The sabbath was made for man, and not man for the sabbath" (Mark 2:27). He claimed dominion over this day, and because it is His day, it is ours also—His gift to us.

Jesus made it clear that the Christian Lord's Day is not a day for idle gossip, for sitting around with hands folded piously. Indeed not! It is a day for good deeds. A day to be kept in the spirit of reverence, service, and worship.

Now we are concerned that this day is at stake in our modern world and society. We need to become aware of that fact. Dr. Leslie Weatherhead, eminent British clergyman at City Temple in London, said in one of his sermons that hardly 10 percent of the English people attend church regularly. Hear his own words: "Unless we take a moral stand for this day, our children will have no Sunday worth talking about."

What, then, shall we do with regard to Sunday? Shall we surrender it, or shall we stand fast in the spirit of Christian witness for it? Are we willing to do battle for it?

Let me point out a few pertinent facts as they have to do with our Lord's Day.

Surely, our physical and spiritual well-being demands that one day in seven be devoted to other than secular pursuits. Our Lord recognized this when He said that the sabbath was made for man. To Him, this was not a day of luxury but of necessity.

Oliver Wendell Holmes once said, "He who ordained the Sabbath loved the poor." In other words, this day was not gotten up by religious fanatics and diehards, but was created by the finger of God. The infinite and eternal Creator knew the need of His creatures for this day.

There is a spiritual rhythm about life, and we get into

trouble when we desert it. Ask the doctors and nurses, as
well as the ministers and psychiatrists who deal with people. They will tell you that one out of every ten hospital
beds throughout America is occupied by the mentally ill.
If the Christian sabbath was needed in the life of yesterday, it is far more needed in our day, with its high pace
of living. Or ask Christian businessmen, of which there
are not a few here in America. They are willing to stand
up and witness for the need of this day. One of them said
to me recently, "Anyone ought to be able to see the common sense value of keeping one day in seven for rest,
recreation, and worship." He added that if we lose our
nerve and let this day go into limbo, then legislation
would be needed to help keep us mentally sane and bal-
anced.

Certainly those who toil and work in the heat of the day
on our modern assembly lines need the Christian Lord's
Day. There is a spiritual and mental rhythm in life which
we desert to our peril. We need to keep the Christian
sabbath holy.

Once, while he was addressing the Lancashire miners,
the great Britisher John Bright quoted the words of
George Herbert: "Without thy light, the week were dark,
Thy torch doth show the way." He was speaking of the
need and place of the Christian sabbath. Not only do we
need to observe one day in seven for the physical and
spiritual well-being of humans, but let us recognize that
those who would scuttle the Christian sabbath are not our
friends, much as they may pretend to be. Nor are they
working for the best interests of the American community.

Many years ago a group of worldly minded men found-
ed a community far out on the West Coast of this nation.
There was one stipulation, namely, that there would be no
Sunday observance. No Christian church. No Christian

minister. Well, they got it, and lived to regret it! What
happened in this wide-open town? Law observance went
by the board. You do not have law-abiding people, apart
from the influence of the church. Property values went
down. People could not get credit in the business world.
No one much wanted to move there. The youth of the
community got into trouble. Home life languished. The
ordinary decencies that make life bearable went by the
board. These hardheaded men eventually admitted their
mistake. They said, "It is clear that we cannot found a
civilized community apart from a Christian church.
We're going to send for the best preacher we can get."
And they did.

In his book *Foundations for Reconstruction*, Dr. Elton
Trueblood tells of the importance of the sabbath in ancient Judah, especially while Judah was in captivity in
Babylon starting in the year 586 BC. Here was a religious
people in an utterly pagan environment. The Northern
Kingdom, Israel, had fallen more than one hundred years
before and had never revived. Only one thing saved the
Southern Kingdom and that was the institution of the
sabbath. Once each week the people stood up as families
to be counted for God. Along with the sabbath came the
institution of the synagogue where people heard the
Word of God read, and were reminded of their primal
loyalties. A precious heritage was saved from extinction
by the observance of the sabbath.

Dr. Trueblood writes that many Americans today are
suffering from "the angelic fallacy." We think we do not
need the supports of institutional religion, that we can get
along on our own. The plain truth is that we are dependent on the loyalties of the past, and that we are not
angels, but men with clay feet.

There are naturally some emergency services that have
to be carried on on Sunday. The faithful doctor must make

his calls, the nurse must care for the sick, the Christian minister must give his sermon and lead his people. Our Lord Jesus healed on the sabbath and He claimed utter dominion over it. We are thinking rather of those secular occupations which are gradually nosing their way into the sacredness of the first day of the week.

You have heard the expression, have you not, "A camel's nose in the tent"? It is the story of the Arab who fetched up one night out on the desert, put up his tent, and, having staked his camel on the outside, lay down to sleep. He had hardly gotten his first wink before the camel came and nosed under the flap of the tent, looked around and thought, *My! How nice it is in there.* Then the camel went a little farther, and got his nose and his front legs in. Soon he got in his hump, and his back legs, until in the last scene we find the Arab on the outside of the tent, and the camel on the inside! It was a complete "takeover."

This camel of secularization has his nose definitely in the American tent. He sells liquor to minors if he can get by with it, and litters our newsstands with pornographic literature. He hawks and peddles his wares over radio, and television, and in our newspapers. He cares not one whit for the moral and spiritual values which constitute the backbone of any civilized community. He wants to scuttle our Christian Lord's Day. He is out for a wide-open sabbath.

You who are parents of small children already know how hard it is to keep a semblance of reverence on a Sunday. I think of that young mother who said to me, "First you battle the Sunday comics, fold the newspaper, and put it away. Then you turn the television off, and get the children scrubbed and dressed. Once in the car you almost break a speed law to get to church on time." Said she, "I made it, but I am almost done in!"

Either Christ is Lord of the sabbath and the sabbath is devoted to Christian ends, or we face the prospect of a godless and lawless nation and society. Only eternal vigilance can preserve what remains of our Lord's Day.

Let us also bear in mind that in this crucial hour of history, with thousands of her sons battling the evil of Communism abroad, America needs the Lord's Day more than ever before.

The late Senator Toby of New Hampshire wrote a book which he entitled *The Return to Morals.* In it he emphasized the need for a return to morals in government and in the world at large. But how are we going to make such a "return" apart from a faithful observance of Sunday? The two main enemies we face in our day are Communism and secularism. Both leave out everything sacred in our heritage: God, worship, the sacredness of personality, the Bible. If you want to know how secularism operates, just look around you. Surely you must be aware of the constant pressure of selfish interests seeking to break down your moral resistance. Many people have become neutral and noncommital in their attitudes. Basic spiritual values gradually dim out.

Do we need to be reminded at this point how Communism works? This evil has taken over area after area of our modern world. On one occasion I talked with a Christian missionary who had been driven out of pre-Communist China. The Communists did not abruptly go and padlock the door of his church. Instead, they called up on Saturday night and informed the missionary that his church building would be needed for other purposes at eleven o'clock Sunday morning. Lenin was right when he said that Christianity and the dialectic of Communism cannot live side by side. Godlessness and Christianity have nothing in common. Believe me, my friends, the Christian sabbath is not a Victorian relic out of the past, to be put in some museum. It is the gift of God to men—one of the few remaining bulwarks standing between civilization on one hand, and barbarism on the other. Truly, Sunday is the core of our civilization!

Here is one incident out of the past which can inspire us to be more militant and loyal when it comes to the preservation of our sacred day. An elderly man once related this experience to Dr. DeWitt Talmadge. He was one of a group rolling across the American prairie toward the [California] gold coast. On Saturday night the covered wagon in which he and his companions were traveling halted at an outpost of civilization. The next day being Sunday, he was invited by the group to spend the day gambling. "I cannot do that," said this man, "for this is the sabbath." The others laughed at him and said, "What do you mean, the sabbath? There is no Sunday out here in the wilderness." "Oh, yes, there is," came the reply. "I brought it with me in my heart across the mountains." And so while the others gambled the day away, he took out his Bible and read, and, like the American serviceman, with whom we began this chapter, he worshiped in that temple not made with hands.

I brought it with me across the mountains!

We began with a question, "Shall we surrender the Christian Lord's Day?" Let us now reply, "We shall not surrender this day. In the name of Him who is Lord of the sabbath, our answer is 'No surrender!' "

*Used by permission, Zondervan, from the book *Faith Alive* by Dr. Aaron N. Mekel.

# 23
# Evidence for Sunday Worship

by Richard W. DeHaan

In every land where the gospel is preached, believers gather in the name of Christ for worship and fellowship. Most of them do so on Sunday, the first day of the week.

A rather small minority of Christendom, however, insists upon keeping Saturday as the weekly sabbath. They tell us we are wrong in gathering as fellow believers on Sunday. According to them, we should observe the sabbath exactly as prescribed in the law of Moses.

Since so much confusion has arisen because of these claims, we have been discussing Sunday, the Lord's Day to clarify the sabbath issue. To begin this lesson, I'd like to emphasize that the Bible does not record a single instance when the Lord Jesus observed the seventh-day sabbath after His resurrection. I realize that this may come as quite a surprise. On the spur of the moment, you might be inclined to question this statement but check your Bible for yourself. You will not find occasion when Jesus, after the cross, recognized and observed the seventh-day sabbath.

On the other hand, every time the Lord met with His disciples after the resurrection, and the day is specified, it was always on the first day of the week. In John 20 we are told. "Then the same day at evening, being the first day of the week, when the doors were shut where the disciples were assembled for fear of the Jews, came Jesus and stood in the midst, and saith unto them, Peace be unto you" (v. 19).

Just one week later, again on the first day of the week, Jesus met once more with his disciples. John told us. "And, after eight days, again his disciples were within, and Thomas with them; then came Jesus, the doors being shut, and stood in the midst, and said, Peace be unto you" (v. 26).

(From Sunday to Sunday, remember, was reckoned by the Jews to be eight days.) Even though we are told that the Lord Jesus appeared to His disciples on the first day of the week on these occasions, nowhere do we find a single word or hint that He ever observed the sabbath after His resurrection. Nor did He even mention the sabbath. This pattern of the Lord Jesus evidently was followed by the believers in the early church. They gathered as a Christian assembly on the first day of the week. They did so by common consent and in commemoration of the Lord's resurrection. Their weekly day of worship was Sunday.

## Evidence from the New Testament

Acts 20 contains a statement that points to the first day of the week as the customary day for the assembling together of all believers. When taken along with Paul's instructions to Corinthian believers about the collection, it strengthens our conviction that believers are to worship on Sunday. The verse says, "And upon the first day of the week, when the disciples came together to break bread, Paul preached unto them, ready to depart on the morrow, and continued his speech until midnight" (v. 7).

Please notice three observations that can be gleaned from these verses. First, the disciples had gathered together on the first day of the week. Second, they assembled for the purpose of breaking bread. Third, Paul preached to them on this occasion. Now read Paul's admonition. "Now concerning the collection for the saints, as I have given order to the churches of Galatia, even so do ye. Upon the first day of the week let every one of you lay by him in store, as God has prospered him, that there be no gatherings when I come" (1 Cor. 16:1-2). This directive was not some isolated local order for the Corinthian church alone. Evidently Paul had given the churches at Galatia the very same instructions. The first day of the week was to be the occasion for the gathering of collections. We may therefore rightly conclude that during the apostolic period believers were assembling for worship and fellowship on the first day of the week and not on the seventh.

I can imagine someone objecting seriously to what I've said, and pointing out the fact that the Book of Acts does record occasions when the apostle Paul went into the synagogues on the sabbath day to preach. I admit that this is true. I also remind you that his preaching in the synagogues on the sabbath day was not directed to assemblies of Christians, but rather to groups of nonbelievers. Paul did not break bread with them, nor did he fellowship with them around the person of Christ. You see, he went into the synagogue on the sabbath day to preach the gospel and to get people saved. When he gathered for fellowship with believers, however, it was on Sundays.

In 1 Corinthians 9, the apostle gave an explanation of his conduct, which also throws some light upon his purpose in going to the synagogues on the sabbath day. Here are his comments: "For though I am free from all men, yet have I made myself servant unto all, that I might gain the more. And unto the Jews I became as a Jew, that I might gain the Jews; to them that are under the law, as under the law, that I might gain them that are under the law"

(vv. 19-20). To win his fellow kinsmen, the Jews, Paul placed himself under the law to win them for Christ.

Remember then, when the apostle went into the synagogues on the sabbath day, he did not go for the breaking of bread or fellowship around the person of Christ. His purpose was to proclaim the gospel.

It is also significant that after Paul finally turned from his own people to the Gentiles, no more mention is made about his activities on the sabbath. The very last time he preached on the sabbath day was recorded in Acts 18.

> And he reasoned in the synagogue every sabbath, and persuaded the Jews and the Greeks. And when Silas and Timotheus were come from Macedonia, Paul was pressed in the spirit, and testified to the Jews that Jesus was Christ. And when they opposed themselves, and blasphemed, he shook his raiment, and said unto them, Your blood be upon your own heads; I am clean: from henceforth I will go unto the Gentiles. And he departed thence, and entered into a certain man's house, named Justus, one that worshipped God, whose house joined hard to the synagogue (vv. 4-7).

These verses contain the last mention of the sabbath day in the Book of Acts. As far as the record goes, this was Paul's final visit to his own people on a Saturday. Having first gone and preached primarily to his own people, the Jews, the apostle Paul turned to the Gentiles, and the sabbath day disappears entirely from the record.

The early Christians met for fellowship and worship on Sunday. They were not under the law of the sabbath. In fact, they were not under legal bondage to any Mosaic law. For that reason, the apostle rebuked those who sought to place believers under the law.

It wasn't easy for some Jewish Christians to break away from the rituals and regulations of their former life. Circumcision, the Temple rites, the rigid distinction between clean and unclean meats, the observance of the weekly sabbath and religious holidays had been a vital part of their lives. They therefore had a strong tendency to carry into their new life certain of those features, and even to demand that the Gentile believers place themselves under some aspects of the law.

This became such a serious problem that on one occasion Paul even rebuked Peter for going along with the legalists. And in Acts 15 we learn that a Church Council was convened for the purpose of determining which aspects of the law should be binding upon Gentile converts. On this occasion Peter said, "Now, therefore, why tempt ye God, to put a yoke upon the neck of the disciples, which neither our fathers nor we were able to bear?" (v. 10).

At the conclusion of that Church Council, the Gentile Christians were advised to abstain from certain things— but not one word was said about keeping the sabbath. This certainly would have been an issue if sabbath-keeping were mandatory.

I think Paul clinched the matter in Colossians 2. Deceivers who had crept into the church were teaching a false asceticism and a rigid legalism. For that reason the apostle Paul found it necessary to write these words: "Let no man therefore judge you in meat, or in drink, or in respect of an holyday, or of the new moon, or of the sabbath days" (v. 16).

## Testimony from Church History

Having observed what the Scriptures indicate about the gathering of believers in the early church on Sundays, we now turn to a testimony from a well-known writer in church history. Justin Martyr was a disciple of Polycarp, a man who had been personally acquainted with the apostle John. He wrote, "Sunday is the day upon which we

[Christians] all hold our communion and assembly, because it is the first day in which God, having wrought a change in the darkness of matter, made the world; and Jesus Christ (our Savior) on that day rose from the dead. And on the day called Sunday, all who live in cities or in the country gather together in one place, and the memoirs of the apostles or the writing of the prophets are read as long as time permits."

We could cite a multitude of other quotations from early church fathers which clearly establish that the first Christians universally worshiped on Sunday.

In spite of all this evidence, however, the charge is sometimes made that Sunday was dedicated to the sun god, and that a mixture of paganism with early Christianity led to its adoption as the day of worship. This contention is supported by lifting parts of sentences out of context from the writings of early historians—a most unethical practice.

The pagan idea had nothing to do with Sunday becoming the Lord's Day! A statement in the *Schaff-Herzog Encyclopedia of Religious Knowledge* explains how it came to be the Christian day of worship. "Sunday . . . was adopted by the early Christians as a day of worship. . . . Sunday was emphatically the feast of the resurrection of Christ, as the Jewish sabbath was the feast of the creation. It was called the 'Lord's Day,' and upon it the primitive church assembled to break bread. No regulations for its observance were laid down in the New Testament . . . nor indeed is its observance even enjoined; yet Christian feeling led to the universal adoption of the day, an imitation of apostolic precedence. In the second century its observance was universal." This is another reason why we worship on Sunday!

## Summary

The recognition of Sunday as the Lord's Day began in New Testament times and has continued down through the ages of church history. The resurrection of the Lord Jesus Christ and the Day of Pentecost occurred on the first day of the week. It soon became the practice of the early Christians to meet together for worship, fellowship, praise, and the study of God's Word on that day. However, it's important to remember that they did not do so to fulfill any legalistic demands, nor had they shifted the sabbath over to Sunday. To speak of Sunday as the Christian sabbath is therefore improper. It is better referred to as the Lord's Day.

Let me remind you that the observance of a day, whether it be Saturday (the sabbath) or Sunday (the Lord's Day) has nothing to do with obtaining salvation. We are not saved by what we do—not even by religious activities or by observing certain days. Salvation just doesn't come that way! The Bible says. "Not by works of righteousness which we have done, but according to his mercy he saved us" (Titus 3:5).

And the Book of Romans declares, "But to him that worketh not, but believeth on him that justifieth the ungodly, his faith is counted for righteousness" (4:5).

The hymn writer so beautifully expressed it:

> Not the labors of my hands
> Can fulfill thy law's demands;
> Could my zeal no respite know,
> Could my tears forever flow,
> These for sin could not atone;
> Thou must save, and thou alone!

Could it be, dear friend, that you have been working at salvation, doing your best, and yet you're not satisfied?

Something is missing. You don't have peace and assurance. Admitting your inability to save yourself—trust the Lord Jesus Christ. Trust Him for your salvation. Receive Him as your Savior. The Bible says, "Believe on the Lord Jesus Christ, and thou shall be saved" (Acts 16:31).*

*Used by permission of the Radio Bible Class, Grand Rapids, Mich.

# 24
# The Lahu and the Lord's Day
by Raymond B. Buker
with Richard Buker

We the twins (Richard and Raymond Buker) were appointed as missionaries to the Lahu and Wa peoples in
Northeast Burma and Yunnan, China, in 1926. A mass
movement had developed among these people during
the previous six or seven years. From a scattering few to
some five thousand a year, these tribal folk were accepting Christ. One missionary team, the Reverend William
Young and his two sons, were the only ones working
among these peoples at this time of Christian growth in
Yunnan. We were sent to them to share in this challenging work. Reverend James Telford was working in Kengtung State with a hospital irregularly staffed in the city of
Kengtung.

In lower Burma, where missionary work had continued
for over one hundred years since the days of Adoniram
Judson, a minority group (the Karens) had accepted Christ
by the thousands. They had a strong indigenous work with
high schools and developing churches. These Karens had
a vision for missionary work and appointed dedicated
workers to go north a thousand miles to work among the
Lahu and the Wa. We would call this home missionary
work; they called it "Foreign Missions," for the Lahu were
people of another language and lived in the wild hills of
Northern Burma.

As Raymond worked alone (no other missionaries and

no one speaking English) with many, many Christians,
illiterate and having no Bibles—not even portions, just a
hymnbook—he realized that these new Christians were
living as they were taught by the missionaries, especially
the Karen preacher-missionaries. Not all at once, but very
slowly, he became aware that the Christian walk of these
new Christians was guided and influenced by the Karen
preachers, who in turn had been schooled by the old
missionaries of lower Burma. These early Baptist missionaries were the product of the church standards and teachings of Christian leaders of New England of 1850. It was
like a church history course. The Karens were taught according to the old New England Puritan standards.

One Sunday the Karen missionary-preacher was talking
to me and posed this question: "Is it right to pick a flower
on Sunday?" I was so surprised and astonished at the question—I wanted to laugh, but I realized he was serious. Out
of the background of his teaching he was honest in his
inquiry. Instead of condemning his narrowness, I tried to
enter into his thinking and basis of consideration for the
Lord's Day. I explained that God had created all these
beautiful things and wanted us to enjoy them seven days
a week.

Perhaps it would be well at this juncture to discuss the
subject of Puritanism. It seems to be the general practice
to criticize and codify a Puritan as a "back number" and
the representative of an unwieldy, impractical heritage,
to be condemned for Christian living. Whereas the Puritan approach can lead one into unhealthy legalism, there
is the opposite side with positive values. The Puritan stood
for something. He was willing to live for and by a clear
standard that encouraged a holy life. The Puritan was
willing to live a life that was in contrast to the carnal,
selfish life that ignores God and His place in our daily
walk. Whereas Puritanism could lead one into habits that

are very strict, tending to emphasize the physical standards of life rather than the spiritual relation to God and His standards, it does have value in developing a yieldedness to the ways and will of God in contrast to physical selfishness.

As time passed, we learned to understand that these early Christians of Burma had been taught a way of life which was held up as the Christian way with Christian standards. It was our responsibility not to be iconoclastic but to build on what they had, leading them into spiritual ways and practices that transcended the legality of the law. They had been taught to observe the Lord's Day as a holy day, and I realized I should beware lest I destroy some of these standards and influence the younger generation into careless regard for God's Day and into the secular modernizing of our Christian life.

The Lahu were a primitive, illiterate tribe of the Tibeto-Burman racial group. They had probably migrated from the north (Tibetan area), settling in the mountains and hills of Western Yunnan and Eastern Burma, in the Shan States area. Their social life was very limited. They were extremely poor, working their fields and gardens from morn till night. Their first meal could be in their home or in midforenoon, consisting of rice which they would carry to the fields. Their second and final meal came after returning from the fields, after dark. There was no evening social life. If the headman had matters of business to perform, the elders gathered in the headman's hut to discuss matters around the open fire.

The only break in this daily work routine was "Bazaar Day." In that part of the world the people gathered every five days to buy and sell whatever was available. The farmers brought their produce; the artisans brought their wares. Much was bartered, but everything was available for cash sales. It was a day when people gathered from all the surrounding villages to learn and pass on the news of the local villages and anything of import from government sources, being passed around by word of mouth. The Chinese might post edicts and judgments, but the people could not read, so they knew only what was told them by word of mouth. When they returned home, such news was passed to the neighbors.

Each bazaar is known by the name of the village where it is held. The bazaars are held in the leading villages of the dominant peoples in the valley or on the plain. Any given Lahu village has two or three bazaars in different directions where the people go for trading and securing supplies. The bazaars are held on different days, the traders going each day to a different bazaar where different clientele from surrounding villages come to trade. The Lahu, according to need or salable products, may also "go to bazaar" in different areas.

This five-day bazaar "custom" is perhaps the most significant feature of the Lahu's social life. The sale of rice beer is perhaps the most negative influence of the bazaar. Heathen Lahu become addicted easily to this type of alcoholic beverage. When the Lahu becomes a Christian, this "drinking of rice beer" is given up and abstinence is a distinctive feature of the Christian Lahu.

When the Lahu becomes a Christian he is taught the basic Christian doctrines. The most clearly evident and understood feature of becoming a Christian, however, is the observance of Sunday. One might think that because of its clarity in the Christian calendar, it would be a simple matter to explain to a new babe in Christ. Upon being examined for baptism, the individual must answer one major question: "Do you promise not to go to bazaar on Sunday?" The answer is always in the affirmative, but the carrying out of this promise is another matter, mainly because they are illiterate people with no calendars.

When the village has a "pastor-teacher" they are able and willing to follow his instructions and leading. Every Sunday is remembered since their teacher is educated and has some sort of a calendar. Mainly, however, he has developed the "Sunday" habit. This is a very special day. All week they have had evening services. After the villagers return from their fields and have disposed of the evening meal, the pastor rings (beats) the gong and the people gather. Of course, there are no street lights, so the people use pine fagots for a torch to light them to the service. This will be held in the church, if they have one, or in the home of the headman, if he is a Christian. There are no electric lights in the church, so the pine fagots are put on a container hanging near the pulpit, This provides light for the pastor to read the Scriptures and dispels the complete darkness of the church. Most cannot read and so do not have a hymnbook.

This evening meeting is held every night, six evenings of the week. Sunday is completely different. No one goes to their fields. They do not have horses or cows. There are no chores such as a farmer would have in America. The pigs run free, as do the chickens. A Christian, however, has a specific schedule. First, there is the "sunrise" service as soon as the sun warms things up a bit, or earlier if the heat of the tropical noonday threatens. At 11:00 AM (sometime before noon) the second service is held. Then in midafternoon, usually by 4:00 PM or before, they gather for the third service. Usually the evening meal comes after that, although the order could be reversed. Because they have no lanterns or lights, they plan this last Sunday service before darkness. This routine makes for the Sunday program. It is very different from the other six days of the week. It is different from anything the heathen Lahu ever do. It is uniquely for the Christian. They like it and easily accept the routine as a special indication of their position as Christians.

In many ways the Christians and non-Christians were the same: they cultivated their fields, harvested their crops, and made trips to the bazaar. However, the non-Christian had no social life except to go to the bazaar. In contrast the Christian schedule was different and they were willing, glad, and ready to have this one day a week for worship which set them apart from the people around them. For those who cared enough to be clear about days in the calendar, it was possible to obtain information from the lunar cycle, the waxing and waning of months, named by the Chinese. Even the year itself was given a Chinese name. But the day of the week called Sunday marked a Christian and gave him something to be proud of.

Perhaps the most noticeable variance from Christian customs occurred when one neglected the observance of Sunday. Some failures were due to ignorance. Often, owing to the poverty of a village, there was no pastor-teacher, and the people did not know how to reckon on a seven-day basis. All their lives they had considered a five-day cycle. So when Sunday fell on a bazaar day, by habit they went to the bazaar. The change in conforming to a seven-day routine required time.

When we compare our culture with theirs and the ease with which our Christian life-style includes Sunday "shopping" on the grounds that we do not want to be "legalistic," we who know better feel very tolerant toward these new Christians seeking to learn a new concept. Sunday, indeed, set the Christian Lahu apart from his neighbors and other Lahu villages where the darkness of evil spirits dominated.

The mission hospital also was distinct from the civil hospital in its observance of Sunday. The mission hospital was not open on Sunday. Emergency cases, of course, were treated. The staff of the hospital, however, were off-duty and were expected to attend church. They were also available for Sunday afternoons to serve as voluntary leaders of the more informal services. This approach was an unwritten testimony to the patients that the hospital staff were Christians, witnessing to the patients, and living a testimony outside of the hospital routine. The patients, a large percentage of whom were not Christian, returned to their homes with a report of what Christianity was, both in doctrine or word, and in example.

Our work included the treatment of a thousand leprosy patients, divided among ten colonies. Each of these centers became a Christian village. At first there was much resentment from surrounding villages. In due time, however, the leprosy villages became respected and appreciated as social contributions in each area. Their Christian testimony in observing Sunday was outstanding. This made the leprosy colonies unique, set apart in a dark and godless world. The example of the Christians brought forth respect and confidence. Week by week they were characterized by their observance of their holy day. It seemed that God honored His followers as they kept His day. He gave them a reputation that was greatly appreciated by their non-Christian neighbors. It was a witness to the world that God honors them that will honor Him!

# 25
# The Sabbath Made for Mankind

by E. Stanley Jones

My friendship with Vaughn and Sarah Shedd is one thing that made me accept this invitation. Then I began to study about the matter. Especially my thoughts began to go to the passage, "The sabbath was made for man, and not man for the sabbath" (Mark 2:27). I began to say to myself, "That isn't off your ground, but right down your alley, the thing you have been thinking about for years." Then I began to be glad that I had been pushed in this direction to redirect another new verse. I share it with you.

We very often twist the verse, "The sabbath was made for man, and not man for the sabbath," into this meaning, "Well, man could do with the sabbath then what he pleases." It was made for him; he was not made for it, to be jammed into it. But the sabbath was made for him; therefore, he can make use of it the way he desires. Thus, the usual interpretation. At least, it becomes the interpretation of our modern world, and a looseness has set in about the whole thing.

I am persuaded that the facts missed the whole point. The sabbath was made for man—that is, it fitted man. It was made because man needed it, demanded it. And the sabbath and man fit each other as light fits the eye, as food fits the stomach, as love fits the heart, and are made for each other. You cannot revolt the sabbath without revolting against yourself, because in the inner nature you are made for quiet rest. What God commands, then, is what nature commands. And the thing that God commands is always the thing that our nature demands. Therefore, the sabbath and man are made for each other.

It is not an arbitrary act of God to say, "Now look here, I want worship, and therefore I am going to tell you that you must set aside one day to worship Me." I have always felt that that was kind of arbitrary and not like the God that I see in the face of Jesus Christ. I have a feeling that God never commands anything that is not our highest interest. The kingdom of heaven, the reign of God is within us. The laws of our being are not other than the laws of God, and when we discover them we discover the laws of God. Now that is one thing that the modern man has got to learn, and is learning it the hard way. He is finding that if one revolts against God, he soon revolts against himself. If he won't live with God, he cannot live with himself. That is the payoff! And the payoff for the revolt against the sabbath is a jittery, jumpy, uneasy age that cannot live with itself. This way of the sabbath is written within us as a demand, and not merely God's command.

I believe that the Christian way is the natural way to live, and that when God commands anything, that is an echo of the demand of human nature. For God didn't command it if we didn't need it. Therefore, wipe out the commands of God and you will find these same demands in your own inner nature. When God says, "Thou shalt not hate; thou shalt love," then look into your stomach and see the same thing written there. You begin to hate and your digestion will go back on you. God said, "Thou shalt have faith and confidence and trust." Look at your nerves and your nerves will say actually the same thing—"Thou shalt have faith and confidence and trust." God said that thou shalt lose thyself, and then thou shalt find thyself coming

back to thyself again. Look into the cells and the cells will
say the same thing. Every cell says, "I have started out to
be the whole, I can be the whole, but I don't. I sold myself
to be the whole. I take a differentiating portion and lose
my life. I serve the rest, and I find myself in brotherhood."

So the Lord Jesus Christ is the law of our own being.
Suppose we say, "But, I don't believe in what Jesus says.
I won't take it. I will do what I like. I can center myself
on myself if I like." Suppose the cell does that, what happens? A cancer. A cancer is a group of cells turned selfish.
They wouldn't serve the rest, they demanded the rest
serve them. Result, a cancer. And they eat their way to
their own death, and to the death of the organs on which
they feed.

What happens to a soul that says that he won't obey the
command of Christ to lose his life, nor to find it again?
What happens? Anything? A cancerous self is a result.
Every self-centered person is an unhappy, cancerous type
of person, eating his way to the death of his own happiness
and to the happiness of the others around him. In other
words, God never commands anything without human
nature demanding that very thing, and made for him, as
the eye is made for light.

Now, we must confess that the Jewish sabbath became
a burden to the Jewish people. It was a legalism and they
thought they had to do it because God commanded it.
And under the fear and trembling of that, they said, "We
will have to do it. It is a burden, but it is a legalism." They
felt it was imposed by the sovereign arbitrary will of God.
We have taken a good deal of that Jewish sabbath over
into our thought of the sabbath.

They tell the story of a boy in Scotland who, when he
came back from church, was scandalized when his dog,
Rover, bounded across the lawn and greeted him with a
bark. "Down Rover, down, don't you know that this's the

Sabbath Day? You not a good Christian at all." And then
he walked out around the house and put his arm around
the donkey's neck, looked into his face, and said, "You are
a good Christian. You got a long, solemn face, just like
Grandpa's; you a good Christian." A great many of us have
looked on it as an imposition of God, and we think we
have to go around with long faces because God commanded it, and we had better submit.

Now, something happened in the New Testament to
take that burden of legalism away. But to rescue the burden, it is a good thing that the Hebrew sabbath didn't
continue. As it was, it was a burden and a legalism. The
Christians couldn't stand that kind of a thing, but they
wanted to keep the core. And they kept the core, and
transferred it around the new creation in the resurrection. So, we don't keep the Jewish sabbath which was
founded on the first creation. We keep the Christian sabbath which was founded on the second creation—a resurrection.

They rescued the sabbath from its bonds and made it
blessed. Yes, they said, "This is a joyous, blessed day, a day
of rest and recreation, but it is connected with victory, not
long faces, not suppression, but the highest expression of
joy and rhythm and harmony that the world's ever seen.
He is arisen!" They connected the Christian sabbath
around that fact, and they do not apologize for that. There
is no point when that took place, it just gradually happened. But before the Christians knew what was happening, they were talking about a new creation, and that new
creation was this resurrected Lord. For the sabbath grew
up around that fact, and that was befitting, because it was
the Christian content that went into the Jewish legalism.

Nevertheless, let me say in passing that it would not be
fair to the Scots to leave that story. I have too much respect for the Scots. I have a little of Scottish blood within

me so I can say that Saint Jerome wrote in the fourth century, "I will remember the Scots in Gaul—they were eaters of human flesh."

Scots! Some people would not like me to say that, but I, as a part Scotsman, glory in the fact that is where we came from. I don't mind where people come from. I am only interested in where they are going. And the Scots go places. And one of the reasons is that they learn to obey something; to subordinate something to higher ends. It might have been a gloomy sabbath, but I tell you that it issued in character and not in mush.

The Scots I have known have contributed something to the world. The Christian sabbath touched here and there by the Jewish sabbath in Scotland has, nevertheless, left a deposit of great character in the Scotch people. They have learned how one day to be quiet and how to listen and to obey. The future is in the hands of those who know how to subordinate a present desire to an end beyond.

Now, we believe they have got to reinterpret the sabbath day in terms of the necessities of human living. What happens if we don't obey the sabbath day, the Christian sabbath? The little girl said, "Grandmother, you know Jesus said to me that to be good is good for me." And she saw something there, that to be bad is bad for me. Now, many of us have the idea that goodness is an arbitrary thing, imposed on us. We have got to do it because God said so. I know God said so because to be good is good for us, and to be bad is bad for us. When God said that thou shalt keep one day and hallow it, He knew we needed that. And He knew that if we did not obey that, we would revolt against ourselves, and we *have revolted against ourselves.*

We have taken these two sabbaths, the Jewish and the Christian, and made a "lost weekend" of them. And the saying goes around now, "It is all right if you don't weaken." And the weekend has become a time of dissipation, and that is the word of energy, of nerves, and a frayed civilization has come out of it. People drive themselves through business up until Friday, and they go off for a weekend, and then drive themselves to try to enjoy themselves. That is the only word I know of, to *drive* themselves, to try to enjoy themselves. And the result is the Monday-morning hangover. Re-creation, recreation—it is the wreck without the creation. More accidents take place on Saturday and Sunday. Why? Muddled with drink; drunk with the lust for pleasure. Men thought they could revolt against God's Day and get away with it, and the Monday-morning hangover is God's hand of judgment they face. I am very sorry you did not take it from the hand of grace; now you have to take it from the hand of judgment.

On a Monday morning I was in a restaurant at 5 AM, and a bleery-eyed man came in and started to sweep up the place. "Oh, he said, "do I hate to go to work!" He had taken the sabbath day. I could see that he had turned it into a day of booze rather than blessedness, and the next morning was the payoff. Monday was now anything but hallowed, and work was anything but hallowed. The whole thing had turned dead on his end because he had broken a law.

No, he did not break a law, *he broke himself on that law!* Therefore, we have frayed nerves. We have frayed bodies. We have a frayed civilization, and therefore, we have a frayed world. We are jumpy because we don't know how to get along with each other. We don't know how to get along with each other because we would not get along with God.

When God said, "Thou shalt not" or "Thou shalt," we said, "Well, I don't know, I will do what I like." We do what we like, and then we don't like what we do. We have our way, and then we don't like our way. That is the payoff in ourselves, and we are getting the payoff right now as a civilization for throwing aside God's sabbath, because this law of rhythm and rest and activity is a law you cannot break without getting broken. If you say that we would let the fields rest and let them have a sabbath, then God says, "I am very sorry, but the fields won't give you what you want," and you have impoverished soil. If you won't take the rest at night, then the next day must be a restless day. It is the rhythm of it—sleep and activity. And if you break that, you break yourself.

I was some time ago on a bus, and I said to myself, *How do these bus drivers live in New York City, driving these buses all day? How do they do it? I wonder why their nerves aren't frayed to a frazzle?* And then I saw how they did it. They run that bus up to a red light, then throw their shift into neutral, and relax. They weren't straining all that time against the red light, waiting for it to turn. They just sat back and relaxed. The moment the green light was on, back they were. But they also had a rest and relaxation in there. So, I said, *I see, every red light becomes a rest.* That is the way to do it. If they didn't rest, they would break themselves in the traffic of the city in record-breaking time.

I used to feel sorry for my heart. I would say to myself, *Good gracious, that pump going on in there has been going on for sixty-six years, and it never stops, never rests. The most amazing pump in the world.* But then I read sometime ago that my sympathy was wasted, that I worked much longer hours than my heart. My heart rests for fifteen hours and works only nine hours a day. Then I said, *I'm not going to be sorry for you. I work longer than that.* But, I tell you, my heart has got some sense. It knows how to rest. But if it kept pounding and pounding without receptivity and without relaxation, we would go to pieces.

I believe that one of the secrets of the Christian life is
to know how to take a quiet time. A sabbath day every day
in Epiphany is that quiet time. One of the most beautiful
things in literature, I think, are those words of Whittier:

> Oh Sabbath rest by Galilee!
> Oh calm of hills above,
> Where Jesus knelt and shared with thee
> The silence of eternity,
> Interpreted by love.

He knelt and shared a sabbath rest and then went out to
interpret it. It was love interpreting God. I believe we
must learn that sabbath quiet of the heart. A person who
impoverishes himself by rushing out into the activities of
the day without a quiet time is going to blow up before
the day is over, and he will spend more time in repenting
than he would have spent in quiet. The uneasiness at
night will more than overbalance what we would have
taken off during the day to be quiet before God.

But a lot of people would rather take aspirin than pray.
If you won't meditate, then you will have to *medicate*. A
lot of people are taking medicine where, if they would
only take meditation, they could drop the medicine. To
be quiet, alone with God, and get resources, to tune yourself alone with Him, to listen, to be receptive—that is the
business of life. And I say to my soul, "If you lose that art,
you have lost the art of living."

A few weeks ago I went to see a dog in New York City.
I had talked about that dog a good deal around the country, and I wanted to pay a personal visit to get to learn
about him firsthand. A pastor and his wife had this dog—a
cross between a Saint Bernard and a collie, a very intelli-
gent dog. At a certain time in the morning, after the
breakfast was over and the children were off to school,
and the dog felt that the housewife had had time to finish

up the dishes, he would stand at the kitchen door and wag his tail, as much as to say, "Now, drop your skillet, you cannot meet New York City without a quiet time; let us go into the quiet time together."

And that dog would stay there, and keep on wagging his tail more furiously, as if she hesitated, as much as to say, "If you don't come and have a quiet time with me, we are going to get into trouble before the day is over." So, she would go into the quiet time with him. He would spread out his paws and lie there perfectly relaxed, while she would have her quiet time with him. And every morning by the clock he would stand there and wait. Now it has become almost artificial, it goes by clockwork. Just the moment she sees him, she knows she has to go.

I told about that dog in another place and a woman came up to me and said, "You know, I have a dog like that. I live on a farm." I found it was a gentlemanly kind of farm. They had raised blooded horses near Philadelphia. "I have a dog that loves to roam the farm with my husband. But when my quiet time comes, that dog will not roam the farm. Whistle, call, but he won't come. He will come into the quiet time with me, will stretch out his paws, and lie there perfectly relaxed, and he and I will have our quiet time together. Then after the quiet time is over, he would be ready to go anywhere: bark, and away he goes across the fields. But he knew that disaster was waiting for him if he didn't have that quiet time, so he had the quiet time."

Now, I would like to lend those two dogs around to harried households, to upset housewives, and cantankerous houses. And if there are any theology students here, I would recommend to them a course in "dogmatics"—getting quiet before God. Incidentally, may I say that the barn burned down on this farm that this lady talked about, and the dog was nervous, excitable, and was getting pan-

icky with all the excitement. And she said that she took
that dog into the room where he always had his quiet
time. When he got there, he just lay there, stretched out
his paws, put his head down, and stayed perfectly quiet in
his place of calm. Then he went to the burning of the
barn. That dog has intelligence—much more than some of
us.

That is what would happen to our civilization. We
would go through our catastrophes and our crises with
quiet and calm if we knew how to keep our sabbath, if we
knew how to get quiet before God, worship, and be receptive. If we don't, then we are going to be a jittery, jumpy,
nervous civilization that won't know how to decide
things. I have often felt that the patron saint of America
is Saint Vitus, and his signs are in jumpy, jittery neon. We
are just getting that jumpy kind of a civilization because
we have lost the quiet time. We have lost the sabbath, and
we are jumping from thing to thing to thing to forget the
emptiness and the laws of God.

Here is what Voltaire said, "If the Christian Sabbath
goes, the Christian religion will be dealt a mortal blow."
There was a time when I would have smiled at that and
said, "I know that would never happen." Now I say that
if the Christian sabbath goes, the Christian quiet goes and
receptivity goes, then God's power is blocked, and the
Christian religion cannot function.

Here is what DeToqueville, the French historian, said:
"America is great and strong because the spirit of the
Pilgrim Fathers has so permeated the people that as a
whole they take one day in seven to stop, reflect and
worship." I wish that were true of our civilization as a
whole. Then we could become great and do great things,
because in the quietness before God, the great issues are
resolved, and great purposes come out. It is the people
who know how to be quiet, and they are the people who

get an activity that knows no exhaustion, that keep on going-power. If we wipe out the Christian sabbath, then we will have to put it back again.

I was in a Russian divorce court where you could walk in and say you wanted a divorce, sign the register, pay five rubles, and it was done *with or without* the consent of your partner. A postcard would be sent to your partner about your divorce. It was done in the lowest biological level. What happened? Russia has discovered what we all have to discover—that the Christian faith is written within us. They are bringing back the Christian family—one man, one woman living together until death parts. They found that their civilization was going to pieces if they didn't put that back.

Statistics tell that the divorce rate in America is now one out of three, a little over three. But today [1950], among church people, it is one out of fifty. Obviously, going to church, being quiet, and listening makes it possible for you to live better with people—if not on account of, then in spite of. So, if we put out the Christian sabbath, it is going to come back again. If we put it out the door, it is going to come back through the window. Out of necessity, the sabbath was made for man, and if man rejects the sabbath, then he rejects himself. If he revolts against the sabbath, then he is going to revolt against himself. And the result is a jittery, jumpy civilization.

I see one more area of the application of the principle— that nobody could run away from God without running away from himself. That outside of God there is nothing but death, and inside of God there is nothing but life, and God's will is our highest interest, and he willed a sabbath for us. Therefore, I believe your institution is founded on a querulous complaint against sabbath breaking, but you are revealing one of the laws of God written into the

nature of things, and I believe therefore that you have
reality behind you. Go forward in God's name!*

*An address delivered by Dr. E. Stanley Jones at the fifty-fifth annual meeting
of The Lord's Day League of New England at Saint Paul's Cathedral, Boston,
Massachusetts, on October 26, 1950. Used by permission of the LDL of New
England.

# 26
# Delight in the Lord's Day

## by Donald C. McHenry

A group of American explorers went to Africa, where they hired native Africans to be their guides. The first day, they rushed along through the jungle in quest of their game. The second day they were up at dawn ready to push again, anxious to get started. They noticed that their African guides were lying very quietly in their places. "Come on," shouted the Americans, "we are in a hurry!" One of the guides replied quietly, "We no go today. We rest. Let souls catch up with bodies." We call Africa the "dark continent." What a wise man this native was. He showed more common sense than most of us.

Do you delight in the Lord's Day? I hope you do. For Christians, this day should have special significance. Like the African who knew the importance of allowing time for his soul to catch up with his body, we need to exercise such wisdom. It is important that we recognize the provisions that Almighty God made for our souls. To honor the Fourth Commandment is essential to our well-being, both spiritually and physically.

We who live in America are blessed indeed. We are privileged to be able to delight in the Lord's Day. Perhaps we take it for granted and it has become so commonplace. It was from an article from the "Voice of America" that the following incident was related:

We have gathered this evening to pray for Sergei Khodorovich. On October 10th of last year we learned that his skull had been fractured as the consequence of torture. Since his arrest in April of last year he had been tortured repeatedly in a cell prepared for that dastardly purpose. The reason for such torture was the nefarious attempt to force him to confess that the Russian Social Fund, which he administered as a volunteer, was financed by the CIA. Because he could not submit to such a lie he suffered greatly. Literally, 'his head was bloody but unbowed.' "

The article continued, saying that laws and amendments in the USSR are aimed at destroying Christian leaders such as Sergei Khodorovich, and also the Russian Social Fund. This is a fund financed by the royalties from Solzhenitsyn's recent book, and established by him when he was banished to Switzerland in 1974. It is the only charitable fund in the Soviet Union. To destroy its work and benefits is to sentence thousands of prisoners' families to starvation and illness. This is a sin against God, against Khodorovich, and against the people of Russia, the article concluded.

The Communist Party newspaper *Pravda* has voiced serious concern about religious influence among minority Soviet populations and called for more vigorous efforts to stamp it out. *Pravda* asserted that Christian churches were involved in sparking crises in Hungary and Czechoslovakia, which brought Soviet military intervention, and were also behind the unrest in Poland in 1980.

Communist Russia works to stamp out worship, the Bible, and the keeping of the Lord's Day. Our gravest peril in America is secularism—the substitution of temporal values for eternal values. It is the replacement of God with mammon. We are seeing the role of religion in the life of our country slowly, steadily diminishing.

## The Bible Upholds the Lord's Day

The sabbath is an ancient and honorable institution. It deserves to be classed with the family, the church, and the state. It is a civil as well as an ecclesiastical institution, contributing much to the strength and happiness of the nation. The sabbath's origin dates back to the dawn of human history. It was here before either the church or the state. It is as early as that primitive institution of society—the family.

*Sabbath* comes from the Hebrew word for *rest.* On this day secular activities give place to activities of the soul. It is the holy day, preempted for religious and spiritual uses. The sabbath's roots are in religion. It has its basis both in revelation and in nature. The word occurs 150 times in twenty Old Testament books; the Greek *Sabbath* is used seventy times in the New Testament, mostly in the Gospels.

God was the first sabbath keeper (Gen. 2:2).

And on the seventh day God finished his work which he had done, and he rested on the seventh day from all his work which he had done. So God blessed the seventh day and hallowed it, because on it God rested from all his work which he had done in Creation (RSV).

God commands in the Fourth Commandment: "Remember the sabbath day, to keep it holy" (Ex. 20:8).

Today the Holy Spirit whispers, or perhaps thunders, in our ears, "Remember the Lord's Day to keep it holy." God knew that people were forgetful, and that these Jews would forget where they had been and what He had done for them without some constant reminder. The sabbath would be a sign between Him and His people. It would remind them that He had created the world, that He had saved them from bondage, and that He had called them to a high and holy task in the world.

In later years, one of the things that preserved the Southern Kingdom of Judah was the observance of the sabbath. Ezekiel, the prophet, sat with them on the banks of the river in a strange land and reminded them of their high calling, and urged them to remember God on the sabbath day. And all the prophets, looking back, knew that much of Israel's greatness came because she had kept the sabbath day, thus remembering God.

I believe it is amazing how faithfully the Jews kept the holy day through the years. In the novel *East River,* one of the main characters is a poor man, who in the closing years of his life wants to observe the Passover once more with his friends. As they gathered together, he spoke these words to them:

> When a man labors not for a livelihood, but to accumulate wealth, then he is a slave. Therefore it is that God granted us the Sabbath. For it is by the Sabbath that we know that we are not working animals—born to eat and to labor—we are men. It is the Sabbath which is man's goal, not labor, but the rest which he earned from his labor. It was because the Jews made the Sabbath holy to God that they were redeemed from slavery in Egypt. It was with the Sabbath that they proclaimed that they were not slaves but free men.

To the Jews the sabbath was to be observed with rest and worship. All work was forbidden to a man, his wife, children, servants, and even the animals. All people were in need of rest. The sabbath was a symbol of God's love for His people, and He wanted this to be a special day, free from ordinary drudgery. The law did not forbid pleasure, so the day became one of feasting. There was no direct command about worship either, but by being quiet, these people began to think seriously about God and life, about God's purpose for His people, and they began to think of the day as a time to build up spiritual reserves. They set up places of worship, and met on the sabbath day to hear the reading of the Word of God, and to strengthen one another in the faith. Interesting to note, such worship, reverence, and thoughtfulness changed the whole tone of their living and changed the whole outlook of the nation.

Strict rabbis drew up a lot of rules over the years regulating everything. Some of these laws were: (1) No work on the sabbath, so a man must be still. He must not shave or ride horseback. If his ox falls in the ditch, he can pull the ox out. If he falls in the ditch, he must stay there. (2) Eggs laid on the sabbath must not be eaten. The hens have been working. (3) If a flea bites a man on the sabbath he must not scratch it, but let it bite in peace, for to try to catch the flea would be hunting on the sabbath.

Once fire broke out in Jerusalem and the Jews, afraid to work, let it burn, and three people were destroyed.

Our Lord was a sabbath keeper. The Gospels present Christ as a sabbath keeper. Luke 4:16 says, "He went to the synagogue, as his custom was, on the sabbath day" (RSV). Jesus ministered to the sick, the suffering, the poor, and needy, performing miracles of healing on the sabbath, stating that "It is lawful to do good on the Sabbath." He reminded the Pharisees who were perverting God's true sabbath, "The sabbath was made for man, not man for the sabbath" (Mark 2:27, RSV). The point he was trying to stress was the fact that the sabbath was made for people—not for money, not for pleasure, not for commercialism, but for people!

The Sunday that we hold sacred was not commanded by Jesus. However, the disciples felt that the resurrection should be appropriately celebrated, and so they transferred their interest in the Jewish sabbath to the Christian Sunday, the first day of the week, the day on which Jesus rose from the dead. Sunday became an official holiday in

AD 321 when Constantine issued a decree saying that it
was to be observed as an official day of rest.

For that reason, the sabbath, our Lord's Day, should be
a gladsome day. As the Psalm writer said, "This is the day
which the Lord has made, let us rejoice and be glad in it"
(Ps. 118:24, RSV) It should provoke happiness and con-
tentment. It should inspire better songs and helps us to
see fairer skies. The day was not intended as a burden, but
a blessing; not as a tax, but a lifting of the load.

We must remember that the sabbath was made for
mankind—not for one person; not for a person; not for
some people; but for all mankind. The Day is not set apart
by us, but by Almighty God. It is not an institution of
earth, but of heaven. It did not come to the world because
Moses in pre-Exilic times wrote it upon clay tablets, but
because God wrote it into human need. God established
the law of the sabbath as surely as He gave the laws of
gravity and of the harvest. All laws in God's sight have an
equal sanctity, and to violate one law is to violate all law.
The Word of God makes it plain—we need to delight in
the Lord's Day.

## What Has Happened to the Lord's Day?

God gives us six days a week for our use and well-being,
to gain and secure what we can. He reserves the remaining days for Himself. What has happened to our Lord's
Day? Our use of Sunday is an indication of a lack of reverence for anything sacred. For many people Sunday is just
a day off from work at the office or plant. It has become
a type of pagan holiday. There are more auto accidents on
Sunday than any other day of the week. Our biggest athletic contests are often held on Sunday. Television has
canceled the place of Sunday night service in many
churches. Many stores and businesses stay open on Sunday just as though it were another day.

I wonder if the church has contributed to this weakening of the impact of the Lord's Day? Has the world squeezed the church into its mold? Many late and great Christian businessmen like J. C. Penney would turn over in their graves if they saw the number of stores which remain open on Sunday and hold their special sales on Sunday.

When many churches began closing down on prayer-meeting nights, then dropped Sunday night worship services, it is no wonder the "world" got the signal that it could move in and take over. I am wondering if the church has been infected by the philosophy that is propagated in our country which says, "Oh, let the government take care of it!" Let the government take over the schools; the government will take over the schools, the hospitals, the social agencies, and the nursing homes, and perhaps sooner than we realize the government will take over the churches.

I wrote to the superintendent of the school district where our youngest boy attends. The school encouraged the various organizations to put on fund drives and gave approval for the fund-raising activities to take place on Sunday. The superintendent's response to my letter was an interesting one. He said, "You know the rest of the community uses Sunday to shop and do business in the mall, along with other local businesses who stay open, thus we in the school are not doing anything different from the others in the valley area." He did not use the word *conform* but that is what he was saying.

Dear friends, God gives us six days a week for our use, and He asks that we honor Him on the one remaining day of the week. Shall we steal that day, too? If Sunday is a human day, then humanity can do with it what it wills; but if it is God's Day, human beings are bound to recognize God's purpose for it. The sabbath, our Sunday, is a divine institution which rests not upon human authorities, but upon the will of God. It is eternal and inviolable; therefore, remember, or better still, take delight in the Lord's Day.

### What Does the Lord's Day Mean?

I remember reading about what the Lord's Day means and I would like to share a few of those ideas that impressed me. First of all, it is a day of rest. "It is sabbath of solemn rest to you" (Lev. 16:31, RSV). You work six days, but on the seventh day you rest. Mankind needs rest each week if people are to work at his maximum capacity.

During World War II my dad worked in a defense plant where they made light tanks. They worked seven days every week. Dad noted that on each Thursday he would begin to lose his momentum. Actually, their productivity declined because there was not a day of rest for the plant workers. Even the Bible speaks of allowing the land to rest for a year so the nutrients could rebuild themselves for greater productivity.

There is the story of the man who brought his mules out of the mines each Sunday. He said that the mules need to stop work and come up out of the mine and darkness or the mules would go blind. Isn't that a marvelous truth? Man can be so consumed in the struggle to make the buck or to enjoy pleasure until he goes blind to the finer things in life.

A story is told of two men at a resort area who used donkeys to take sightseers to the top of a high mountain. The donkeys belonging to one man looked well and strong. The donkeys belonging to the other were scrawny and worn looking. Asked why, the first man said he sent his donkeys six days a week, and gave them one full day for rest. The other man indicated that he sent his seven days a week with no rest. The moral of the story is simple:

even a jackass knows that one day in seven ought to be a day of rest.

We need time to think about the things in life that really matter. We must consider the things that are more important than making money, having fun, or being famous. These all pass away. If we are never still and never rest, we miss the important things in life. The Lord's Day —properly observed—will help us regain the physical strength needed for using the balance of our time in making a good name, and in making some worthwhile contribution to the life of the world.

Second, it is a day of worship. A proper observance of Sunday requires time spent in worship, public worship. People cannot live fully without associating with other people in public worship. Isaiah the prophet said (56:1-2),

> Thus says the Lord: "Keep justice, and do righteousness,
> for soon my salvation will come,
> and my deliverance be revealed.
> Blessed is the man who does this,
> and the son of man who holds it fast,
> who keeps the sabbath, not profaning it,
> and keeps his hand from doing any evil" (RSV).

I am sick and tired of hearing people say they can worship as well on the golf course, at a picnic, or lying on the beach as they can in church. The truth is: when you are on the golf course, you are thinking of golf. When you are at a picnic, you are thinking of food. When you are lying on the beach, you aren't thinking!

I realize that the preacher can make it dull to come to church and listen to a sermon. A preacher was visiting his shut-ins and one elderly lady was bemoaning the fact that she couldn't go to church and hear the sermon. The preacher, to console her, said, "Lady, you aren't missing anything." She replied, "That's what everybody tells me."

No matter how sorry the sermon may be, it is vital to be in worship each Lord's Day. To be with the people of God and to participate means you are hearing God's Word read aloud. You sing the great hymns of the church which stir the soul. Sitting prayerfully through the prayer time stimulates the mind with thoughts of God. Listening to the choir lifts the soul in adoration. Being with others who also are seeking spiritual truth encourages your own search for finding God. These things make church attendance worthwhile, essential to our well-being.

We need the experience of worship to help recreate our spirits. Men, women, young people, and children who worship regularly aren't easily overcome with the problems of life for they have found a Source of strength that none other knows. Our spirits are renewed and we gain strength for the long road ahead. We need the experience of worship because life often gets our goat.

Do you know the history of that expression? It seems that racehorse owners often put a goat in the stable with sensitive, high-strung horses. It helps to quiet them. The presence of the placid goat helps the horse to relax. Sometimes, just before a race, an unscrupulous owner would steal the goat out of his rival's stable. He knew that if he succeeded in "getting his neighbor's goat" his horse would not run as well in the next day's race.

Too often, life does get our goat. We live with jangled nerves. It is no wonder that our mental hospitals are filled, it is no wonder the drug manufacturers sell millions of sleeping pills every day. Our problem is that we have not made use of one simple thing that will help us keep our tranquility and our sanity: Worship!

Last of all, Sunday is a day of service. The Gospel writer (Mark 3:1-2) tells of Jesus and how He used the sabbath in His day. "Again he entered the synagogue, and a man was there who had a withered hand. And they watched him, to see whether he would heal him on the sabbath, so that they might accuse him" (RSV). Jesus gave us an example. He used the sabbath for doing good.

What can we do? Why not call on the sick, the lonely, or those in sorrow? What better way to spend the Lord's Day than in bringing them help? We get so busy with our own affairs that we forget to be kind. What a great opportunity Sunday brings us to do some extra, positive good for people, for the church. Jesus made the final criterion of life a simple one after all: "Inasmuch as ye have done it unto one of the least of these my brethren, ye have done it unto me" (Matt. 25:40).

Actually, Sunday comes as a judge. The use to which we put our Sundays is a test of what we are and what we think is important in life. Someone said that what you do with six days a week determines what you live on. What you do with Sunday determines what you are. My friends, do you delight in the Lord's Day? I pray you do and that you will continue to remember the Lord's Day.

# 27
# The Fourth Commandment

### by W. Wyeth Willard

For most Christians the Fourth Commandment is rather lopsided. "Remember the sabbath day, to keep it holy" (Ex. 20:8) is the most favored view of the coin. But: "Six days you shall labor and do all your work" (v. 9, RSV) to most Christians is the ignored or utterly neglected side of the same divine coin, which was minted in heaven.

What is work? A dictionary states as follows: "physical or mental effort exerted to do or make something; purposeful activity, labor, toil." It is interesting to note this fact: the very first time in recorded history that God spoke to mankind, He gave the progenitor of the human race a job, at which he was commanded to work. This was a command in which mankind had no choice whatsoever! He either obeyed and won the praise of his Maker, or he disobeyed and lost the blessing.

God gave mankind his first assignment:

> Be fruitful and multiply, and fill the earth and subdue it; and have dominion over the fish of the sea and the birds of the air and over every living thing that moves upon the earth (Gen. 1:28, RSV).

The Bible mentions mankind's work schedule long before the sabbath law was enacted. Work precedes rest. Amen.

In many passages throughout the Bible, the subject of

work and the achievements of God's outstanding employees are recorded for posterity.

Without a doubt, the most gifted worker portrayed in
the Old Testament was Moses. What a great man of God!
For forty years he was "the son of Pharaoh's daughter,"
a real "Somebody!" For the next forty years he was the
humble servant of Jethro, his father-in-law. For the last
forty years he was a worker for God. When the Hebrew
people finally settled in the Promised Land, they labored
with great dedication to build a strong and godly nation.

In the year 598 BC the armies of Israel were defeated
and the Hebrews were taken into Exile in Babylon. Some
decades later they were permitted to return to their native land. The prophet Nehemiah encouraged the people
through hard work to rebuild the destroyed walls of
Jerusalem. The prophet Haggai urged the Hebrews to
repair the Temple in Jerusalem that had been demolished
by the enemy. They were decorating their own homes,
but were neglecting the holy Temple. "Work, for I am
with you, says the Lord of hosts, according to the promise
that I made you when you came out of Egypt" (Hag. 2:4-5,
RSV).

Jesus came into the world not as a mere observer or an
idler but rather as a worker par excellence. He gave three
years of His short life to evangelistic tours, augmented by
an intense teaching ministry. He directed a series of open-
air clinics. He catered meals to thousands of hungry people. He performed stunning miracles. He was an able
debater. He gave sympathetic counsel to multitudes. He
prophesied of "things to come." He was an eloquent and
inspiring preacher.

When He was tortured, He forgave His tormentors.
Humanly speaking, at the end of His three years of ministry He must have been physically, intellectually, and emo-
tionally exhausted. No human being of ancient or in

modern times has ever accomplished so much in so few years as did Jesus of Nazareth.

The secret of His success? He had supernatural powers. He was the Son of God incarnate. But beyond all His divine attributes as God in the flesh, born of the blessed virgin Mary in the household of a carpenter, as a human being Jesus was a hard and seemingly tireless worker.

There is an ancient poem that goes like this:

My Master was a worker;
    a workingman was He;
And we who would be like Him,
    must also workers be.

In John's Gospel alone, the word *work* appears in several forms twenty-three times. Jesus said, "We must work the works of him who sent me, while it is day; night comes, when no one can work" (John 9:4, RSV). When Jesus was looking forward to His death upon the cross, he prayed to the Father, "I glorified thee on earth, having accomplished the work which thou gavest me to do" (John 17:4, RSV).

God's beloved Son ordained His followers, then and now, young and old, that they should become workers. Jesus told His disciples, "Truly, truly, I say to you, he who believes in me will also do the works that I do; and greater works than these will he do, because I go to the Father" (John 14:12, RSV).

Christians who wish to please the living Christ, must of necessity become workers. Idleness; the playboy life; self-adoration; lusting after riches, pleasure, or fame; all these lesser things will surely never earn the words of the Master on that great day of His appearing, when He shall pronounce to those on His right hand, "Well done, good and faithful servant" (Matt. 25:21, RSV).

Notice that Jesus uses the words "well done," not what

one has dreamed of doing, or wished to do, or promised to do, but what has been accomplished. Servants of King Jesus are His workers, not shirkers.

The sacred Scriptures record that the early Christians were workers. The ordinary church members (along with the apostles) as Spirit-filled individuals proclaimed the gospel by word and deed.

> A great persecution arose against the church in Jerusalem; and they were all scattered throughout the region of Judea and Samaria, except the apostles [the pros]. . . . those who were scattered went about preaching the word (Acts 8:1,4, RSV).

Note the apostles remained in Jerusalem, but the "lay-persons" went into the provinces preaching the gospel.

Paul the apostle was a worker without parallel in the annals of mankind. While he carried on a successful tent-making business by which he earned his living, he took time out of his secular occupation to hold evangelistic meetings in Jewish synagogues, or in open-air services in public places, or aboard ship, or in large cities, or country places, or at the homes of believers. He was responsible for the founding and nurturing of many churches. He wrote epistles which have become classics in theological seminaries throughout the world. Paul was not only a man of God, but above all he was a tireless worker.

In the centuries following the founding of the Christian church in Jerusalem, thousands of men and women have been engaged in obeying Jesus by spreading the gospel in all the world. Men like Luther, Calvin, Knox, the Wesleys, and countless others, have literally worn themselves out "in the harness" for the gospel's sake.

Notice that God's command has no limitation as to age. According to tradition, John the apostle wrote the gospel bearing his name when he was an aged man. His disciple

Polycarp was eighty-six years old when he was burned to death as a martyr.

"Six days shalt thou labor" does not mean that a minister or a missionary must of necessity stop working at age sixty or sixty-five to await a heart attack and the undertaker, or to just fluff off into eternity.

In recent years, many clergymen living on pensions have offered their services to churches and mission agencies as volunteer, unpaid workers at home or abroad. Some pastors, in the larger or even in the smaller churches, could use dedicated volunteer helpers for the spread of the gospel.

Oldsters are happiest when they are occupied with worthwhile projects. One such minister, who had given his professional years as a pastor, after retiring volunteered to serve under the auspices of a mission board in Africa. He labored hard and with excellent results until he died (in the harness) in his nineties. The example of that man inspired his loyal and admiring son, Foster McGaw, founder and president of the American Hospital Supply Corporation of Chicago, to give several million dollars to Northwestern University in Evanston, Illinois, for the erection of the McGaw Memorial Building.

God has ordained that man should labor—and that with no time restrictions. Young people as well as senior citizens are happiest when they feel that they are wanted, that they are needed, and that they can accomplish something for family, for country, and for God, by laboring for a great cause. What cause is more imperative than that of spreading the message of Jesus into all the world until "the earth shall be full of the knowledge of the Lord as the waters cover the sea" (Isa. 11:9*b*, RSV).

"Work, for I am with you," says the Lord. Yes, and work so hard that the one day of rest in seven becomes a delightful and heavenly oasis in the journey through life.

The preceding paragraphs are but one side of the coin. The other side, "Remember the sabbath day, to keep it holy," was given by God to mankind for several reasons, among which is this: A person who loves God should work so hard for six days that, of necessity, without any urging, the seventh day is spent in a relaxed atmosphere of rest, joyous worship, and the cultivation of the mind.

The Fourth Commandment, as set forth by the voice of God speaking to Moses on Mount Sinai, stated plainly "Six days you shall labor and do all your work; but the seventh is a sabbath to the Lord your God" (Ex. 20:8-9, RSV).

The first part of this study considers the work ethic as applied to those persons who hear and comply with regulations set down in the Word of God.

The second part briefly, and not by any means exhaustively, examines the meaning of the sabbath.

First of all, one day in seven is set aside. In citing the seven days of the week in Genesis 1, it cannot be alleged that those seven days consisted of twenty-four hours duration each. The sun in the solar system was not set in place until the fourth day of Creation Week. Therefore the first three "days" of creation might be thought of as a thousand years, ten thousand years, or longer since the Hebrew word *yom* for *day* in Genesis could mean a long period of time.

We may assume, but have no way of knowing for sure, that the traditional Hebrew sabbath as established by Moses in the desert of Mount Sinai, fell on Saturday. According to requirements for temple worship in the wilderness, for the clergy Saturday was a workday. In all fairness, the Hebrew priests deserved one day per week for rest. Logically this rest day might have fallen on the day after the people's sabbath, or on Sunday.

On the Hebrew sabbath, all buying and selling, all labor in the fields were halted (Neh. 13:15-23). The slaves and their supervisors rested from their toil. The dwellers in their cities and villages gathered in their synagogues to worship the God, who by His mighty arm had saved their forefathers from slavery and made them free.

In the days of Jesus the Messiah, He and His disciples kept the sabbath day. They made it not simply a time for bodily rest, but also a day for performing good deeds. One of the choicest stories in the New Testament is the narrative of how the bighearted Jesus healed the man with a withered hand on the sabbath day (Mark 3:1-9).

Careful study by modern scholars discloses the fact that we know of a certainty that the Jewish sabbath fell on Saturday, which according to the calendar of that day, was the seventh day of the week. Saturday then is the Saturday of today. We also know for a certainty that the first day of the week (Sunday) in Jesus' time is also the first day of the week in our modern age.

According to church historians, in the centuries of the Christian era up to AD 500, there were even then Christians who observed the Jewish sabbath. By the middle of the fifteenth century, many Jewish converts secretly or under some pretext, still kept the sabbath, the Passover seder, and synagogue observances.

In this twentieth century, there exists a flourishing Seventh-Day Adventist denomination, the Seventy-Day Baptists, and others, who with the modern Jewish peoples, choose to worship on Saturday. The doctrine of soul liberty, as first espoused by Roger Williams of Rhode Island, that pioneer of religious freedom in our modern world, covers and protects them from the darts of would-be persecutors and detractors.

Actually, people around the world cannot rest and worship at exactly the same time and on exactly the same day. Why? Because at the international date line between Siberia and Alaska, a traveler can put the left foot in one

place on Sunday and the right foot across the line on
Saturday.

Is there a possibility of uniform conformity of sabbath
observance around the world? Certainly not!

Therefore, we return to our Old Testament age for a
brief heart-to-heart talk with Moses as follows: "Moses, did
God intend for all the people in all the world to observe
a sabbath at the same hour on the same day of the week?"

We have no right to put words in the mouth of that man
of God. His brother Aaron might have answered as follows: "You dolt, don't ask foolish questions."

But we do have applicable words from one called the
Second Moses. Jesus of Nazareth once said, "It is the spirit
that quickeneth" (John 6:63). The Spirit of the sabbath
enables the missionaries, the priests, the pastors, the evan-
gelists, and other church workers to have one day off in
seven. For many of the clergy, Monday is that day. Perhaps that explains the origin of the name "Blue Monday."

So, what about our Sunday laws of the present age?

For the majority of Americans and citizens in the Christian nations of the world, Sunday has a double significance: first as the accepted common day of rest; and
second, as the day certified by five hundred Jewish wit-
nesses (1 Cor. 15:6) that Jesus Christ literally rose again
from the dead. So the argument for sabbath observance
alone is flying on one wing, the common day of rest for the
vast majority of citizens, believers and unbelievers alike.
But from the universally regarded point of view, as held
by Roman Catholics, Protestants, and the various Ortho-
dox bodies, the observance of Sunday flies on a second
wing. It was the first day of the week when the greatest
miracle of the New Testament was performed: Jesus
Christ rose again from the dead, the only such incident in
recorded history.

What about the law of the land?

Sunday laws in the various states of America have been tumbling down. What should the Christian people of our country do? Only cowards and weak-kneed pseudobelievers give in when the spiritual conflict gets hot.

The famous World War I French general, Ferdinand Foch, once said, "We advance when we attack."

All Christians on all fronts in America should join the battle with renewed vigor. The leaders of our denominations, the pastors of churches, and civic leaders should hear from all persons who believe in and love our Lord and His day. In proposing sabbath legislation, citizens who worship on Friday or Saturday or any other day of the week should be protected. The reasons for retaining Sunday as a common day of rest, a day for family culture, for good deeds, for worship, should be reinstated as follows:

1. All human beings need one day off each week for relaxation and rest.
2. Christians who worship on Sunday ought to be exempt from secular activities on their sabbath.

I hereby submit a battle plan. We believe, don't we? We have faith, don't we? We accept the miracles of the Bible as a part of history, don't we?

Why not start right now a Christians United Society? Dues could be two or three dollars per year. The Headquarters could be in Atlanta, Georgia. The pledge: I promise to observe the Sunday as our sabbath. On the sabbath day I promise not to engage in buying or selling, or patronizing the stores, unless extreme necessity compels me to do so (or any other appropriate pledge).

Start with two charter members. Double the number each year. In ten years 1,024 persons would have joined. There would be losses through death and defection. In twenty years the number would reach 2,097,032, less losses. In twenty-seven years the number would reach 268,740,096 persons throughout the world, less losses.

Impossible? Nothing is impossible at Mount Calvary.

I'd rather try and fail, than not try at all. But with God all things are possible.

We advance when we attack!

# 28
# Perplexing Questions About the Lord's Day

by James P. Wesberry

When I mail an envelope I never stick one of those "happy face" stickers on it. I'm not opposed to smile stickers. I like them. I have what I think is a better idea. I attach a bright yellow sticker (about the same size and color of the usual "happy face") which, I believe, will bring more happiness if its advice is followed. The sticker I put on every envelope that leaves my office says this: "We prefer to shop at stores that close on Sundays."

This sticker is one way of answering a question I am frequently asked. "What can we do about the observance of Sunday?" My sticker is only one answer. There are other answers. Yet, let's start with the questions, perplexing as they are.

Perhaps you are seeking some answers to these questions: Must the Christian obey the sabbath? How can I pass along positive attitudes to my children and grandchildren without sounding legalistic? What does the New Testament teach about the Lord's Day? Why Sunday and not Saturday? If I believe in honoring the Lord's Day, how can I turn my belief into action?

I hope to answer some of your questions. I have developed it from a lifelong study of God's Word on the subject.

## Must a Christian Observe the Sabbath?

God, the great, divine Lawgiver, considered the sabbath to be of the utmost importance. He placed it fourth among the Ten Commandments and gave it more space than any of the others. It is high on the list of divine priorities.

We might well ask ourselves, "How important is it to us? What place does it have among our priorities? Does it encourage laziness?"

The sabbath is God's golden gift to humanity. It was made, Jesus said, "for man, and not man for the sabbath" (Mark 2:27). It was made to fit human need.

I can't get used to the current saying, "Thank God, it's Friday." I've always loved my work and never wanted to take a break from it. I'm in the minority here; many don't feel as I do. I meet auto mechanics and bank clerks who hate their jobs and dream of quitting.

God intended for people to work. Indolence is a cardinal sin. Idleness, not work, can be a curse. Every ablebodied person should work, or, as the apostle Paul said, "neither should he eat" (2 Thess. 3:10).

But as important and necessary as work is, God never intended for people to work all of the time. All work and no rest robs life of zest, enthusiasm, and vitality. No matter what kind of work you do, whether with brawn or brain, you need rest.

The Bible tells us that, after making heaven and earth, the sea, and all that is in them, God "rested the seventh day" (Ex. 20:11). By having one day in seven as a day of rest, persons can accomplish far more in six days than they can by working seven.

Frayed nerves, broken bodies, bad health, and premature death often come from driving oneself at full speed day and night without rest.

The sabbath is a Godsend to all who labor and to all whose time is not their own. We are told that the slaves of the old South used to sing: "Every day will be Sunday by and by." Sunday was the day when the heavy load was lifted off their shoulders, and they could contemplate eternal rest.

Times have changed, and some people deliberately try to forget the sabbath. They do it intentionally; they desire pleasure; they want money. The sabbath gets in their way. For many selfish, sinful reasons, people forget to remember the sabbath day and to keep it holy. They prefer to keep it in their own way: buying and selling—business as usual.

For many people the sabbath no longer is a holy day but a holiday, a day for pleasure, recreation, playing, hunting, fishing, boating, swimming, riding, going on trips, baseball, football, movies, concerts, visitation of relatives, and forgetting all responsibilities. For pleasure seekers and money lovers, the sabbath is anything but a holy day.

People need guidance. Christians with perplexing questions want answers. Among many questions asked about the sabbath, perhaps the most important is not "What may I do or not do on the sabbath?" but "How may I make the most of this day for Christ?"

Is it really the Lord's Day? Yes, all days are His. All days are holy. We are to use every day for Jesus, but Sunday is His special, unique day. If Christ is the Lord of your life, your relation to Him will determine your attitude toward the use of this special day. You will use it as He used it—for the glory of God and in the interest of the human race. You will use it not only as a day of rest and relaxation but also as a day of worship and Christian service. This is the highest, holiest, and most rewarding use you can make of the Lord's Day.

Our Savior Jesus Christ enlarged, sanctified, and enno-

bled the sabbath day. He set it free from the bondage of
Pharisaical traditions.

One sabbath day, as Mark records (2:23-24), Jesus and
His disciples walked through a grain field. As one who has
served as pastor and preached in many country churches
I have walked in many corn fields and a few wheat fields—
sometimes on the Lord's Day. Perhaps you have, too. We
may be absolutely sure that Jesus was on an important
mission. He never idled time away. His disciples pulled
several grains of wheat or barley and rubbed them between their hands to loosen the kernels.

We see nothing unusual about this. But, as strange as it
may seem, Jesus' bitter Pharisaical enemies saw it and
complained "Why do they on the sabbath day that which
is not lawful?" They didn't blame Jesus directly, but His
disciples. The Pharisees demanded Him to answer for
them. The critics didn't accuse them of stealing or violating property rights; according to Deuteronomy 23:25 the
law permitted such freedom.

According to the absurd exaggeration of the law, it was
a violation. The Pharisees thought of plucking these
grains as a kind of "reaping" and the rubbing of grains as
a sort of "threshing" on the sabbath. Reaping and threshing were among the thirty-nine kinds of labor forbidden
on the sabbath by the law. Legalists gave minute directions on the observance of the sabbath, and their many
meticulous traditions had transformed the joyous sabbath
into a burden to be borne. Some of their traditional laws
were really humorous and ridiculous. The Pharisees made
a person a slave to the sabbath. Jesus opposed their traditional observance of the sabbath day. The sabbath, Jesus
taught, is a person's servant.

By the time Jesus was born, the Jews had interpreted
the Mosaic law in an absurd, meticulous way. The Jewish
religious teachers had derived more than fifteen hundred

rules of conduct designed to regulate sabbath observance. "No work" was interpreted as "no carrying of burdens." This meant "no ribbon pinned on the dress—that is a burden. It must be sewn on—then it is part of the dress." False teeth must not be worn on the sabbath. That was wearing a burden. A woman must not use a mirror on the sabbath. She might see a gray hair and pluck it out. If she did, that was "reaping" and was a violation of the sabbath. They made the day more of a burden than a blessing. Is it any wonder that Christ called the Pharisees hypocrites and said, "The sabbath was made for man, and not man for the sabbath"? Jesus liberated the sabbath from traditionalism.

The sabbath is given for human benefit. It is made for human enjoyment, just as light, air, food, and water are. The sabbath is for human use under the lordship of Christ —"Therefore the Son of man is Lord also of the sabbath" (Mark 2:28). The sabbath is subject to the Son of man and the right to modify and control it belongs to him. He is most emphatically the Lord of the sabbath. Christ's disciples are not to be shackled by the Pharisees' traditions but are subject to the guidance and direction of Jesus Christ their Lord.

People of the early church took these words as encouragement about Jesus' lordship over the legalistic observances. They felt free to turn from the narrow, restrictive views of the Jewish holy day and to center their attention on the first day of the week. Church history records that in AD 110 the feeling was already strong to disregard the seventh day and celebrate the Lord's Day.

## Is My Example Important?

On March 21, 1977, I wrote to President Jimmy Carter, telling him about a unique resolution passed by the board of managers of The Lord's Day Alliance of the United

States. Our organization urged the president and congress "to avoid the use of Sunday for transacting business"
and to enact legislation "to protect one day in seven as a
day of rest and renewal for the people of our nation."

On November 15, 1977, I received a letter from the
president's special assistant saying: "The best the president can do in this area is to set an example, which he
does. As you know, the president attends church regularly
and does not schedule official events on Sundays. Most
Sundays are devoted to church and family."

For this response we were most grateful. It was indeed
a beautiful and inspiring example.

Just as a president considers his example, a parent or
grandparent should try to be a role model. If we really
want to know how to keep the Lord's Day in the Lord's
way, let us look at Jesus. Jesus set the perfect example for
us to follow in keeping the sabbath day as it should be
kept. Jesus put into practice in His own life what He
preached about the sabbath.

One day Jesus went back to His old hometown of
Nazareth. He had grown to manhood there. If you have
ever visited Nazareth, maybe you have seen the tourist
attraction they claim is the place where Jesus lived as a
child and where Joseph had his carpenter's shop.

Jesus had grown in popularity and fame. His name was
on the lips of many people. Every eye was watching Him.
Little children, young people, and men and women of all
ages were attracted to Him. It was rumored that He
would be at the synagogue on the sabbath day. They all
wondered. Many hoped to see Him.

The Scripture says that it was the habit of Jesus to attend instruction and worship: "As his custom was, he went
into the synagogue on the sabbath day" (Luke 4:16).

Jesus probably never missed worship on the sabbath
day. It is impossible to think of His absenting Himself

from the Father's house on the sabbath day. We cannot
imagine His finding excuses for sleeping late or using the
day for trivial amusements.

What a wonderful example any of us could set! I will
never forget one of my deacons in a church in South
Carolina many years ago. He was stone deaf. He couldn't
hear it thunder—but he was always in the worship services. Somebody asked him one day why he kept coming
since he couldn't hear anything the pastor said. He quickly replied, "I have two sons." This is an excellent reason
for attending worship, but the supreme reason should
always be because of our great love for Christ our Savior
and in joyful, thankful celebration of His glorious resurrection from the grave.

Worship brings the soul in touch with the Unseen. It
cleanses our stained and sinful lives. In worship we dedicate ourselves to the highest, holiest, noblest aims and find
comfort, peace, and strength. "They that wait upon the
Lord shall renew their strength" (Isa. 40:31).

Jesus set the perfect example in worship. But He did
more.

On another sabbath, He healed a man with a withered
hand. To those who criticized Him, He said, "What man
shall there be among you, that shall have one sheep, and
if it fall into a pit on the sabbath day, will he not lay hold
on it, and lift it out?" (Matt. 12:11). He taught that a
human life is of far more value than a sheep and that it
is perfectly legitimate to exercise an act of mercy and
necessity on the sabbath day.

There was also a woman who for eighteen years had
suffered a spirit of infirmity. She could not lift herself up.
"He laid his hands on her: and immediately she was made
straight, and glorified God" (Luke 13:13). The ruler of the
synagogue blamed Jesus for doing this on the sabbath day,
but Jesus said,

Thou hypocrite, doth not each one of you on the sabbath
loose his ox or his ass from the stall, and lead him away to
watering? Ought not this woman, . . . whom Satan hath
bound, lo, these eighteen years, be loosed from this bond
on the sabbath day? (vv. 15-16).

Notice the effect of Jesus' rebuke upon them: "And
when he had said these things, his adversaries were
ashamed" (v. 17).

Many visitors who travel the Via Dolorosa in Jerusalem
in modern times turn aside to the Pool of Bethesda. There
they find written in 135 languages the lovely story of "The
House of Mercy," the real meaning of Bethesda. There
was a traditional belief that when an angel caused the
waters to bubble, the first person to get into the pool
would be healed. One poor man who had been crippled
for thirty-eight years had tried many times but was never
able to reach the pool. He had no one, when the waters
were troubled, to help him in. One sabbath day Jesus
came by and healed this poor man. In the place of misery
and suffering, Jesus built a house of mercy.

Jesus showed clearly that He believed a human life to
be greater than the sabbath. He never lessened the obligation of the sabbath but emancipated it from Pharisaical
sanctimonism. Instead of destroying it, He brought out its
deepest meanings. He showed that by His own example
that it is not wrong to do work of necessity. We should, as
He demonstrated, do all the good and bestow all the acts
of mercy we can any day, whether it be on the sabbath or
during the week.

## What Does the New Testament Teach About the Lord's Day?

### Why Sunday and Not Saturday?

One of the questions that has given many people much concern is why did Christians come to worship on the first day of the week. Why the first instead of the seventh day? How did this change come about from Saturday to Sunday?

Practically all scholars are agreed on this point: the first day was celebrated by Christians as a joyful festival of the resurrection of Jesus Christ from the grave. Sunday observance is grounded in the Easter event.

Even though you will find similarities, note the differences in the two days. The seventh day was observed by the Israelites in memory of the rest day of God after creation and in memory of their deliverance from Pharaoh's cruelty. The first day of the week is observed and honored as the Christian sabbath in grateful and loving remembrance of our Lord's resurrection from death and His triumph over the grave.

The old sabbath commemorates the first creation, the beginning; the Christian sabbath commemorates the new beginning in Jesus Christ. The Jewish sabbath symbolizes deliverance from bondage; the Christian sabbath symbolizes deliverance from the bondage of sin.

Saturday was the sabbath of nature: Sunday is the sabbath of grace. Saturday is the sabbath of a rejected, executed, entombed Jesus; Sunday is the sabbath of a risen, exalted, triumphant Christ. Saturday is the Creator's day; Sunday is the Redeemer's day.

Those who insist that we should be able to quote a direct command of Jesus that "The Lord's Day" replaced the old Jewish sabbath are reminded that Christ's actions speak as loudly as His words. His acts are as authoritative as His teachings. As the Lord's Supper replaced the Passover meal, as Christianity largely displaces Judaism, the Christian sabbath displaces the old sabbath. Jesus changed the meaning and purpose of it.

Our Lord not only rose from the grave on the first day of the week but He also made repeated visits to His disciples on that day. All the Gospel writers tell us that He rose on the first day. Five times that very day He showed himself to His disciples. On the first day of the following week, He appeared to His disciples again in the upper room.

While the Scriptures tell us that during His lifetime Jesus worshiped in the synagogues on the sabbath, we have no record that during His resurrected forty days on earth He did so. The record shows that He honored the meeting of His disciples on the first day.

The most important event in the history of the early church next to the resurrection was the coming of the Holy Spirit at Pentecost. Pentecost likely came not on the seventh but on the first day of the week. It was the fulfillment of ancient prophecy (Lev. 23:15-16). Jesus honored the early church by establishing it on the first day of the week. What a day it was! It was the beginning of church history. On that day of the week, the first gospel sermon on the death and resurrection of Jesus was preached by the apostle Peter (Acts 2:14-40). On that same day, three thousand people gave their hearts to Christ, received baptism, and were united in the first New Testament church. The sacred ordinance of Christian baptism was first administered on that day (v. 41).

On the first day of the week, the apostles preached at Troas where the disciples had come together to break bread. Paul tarried there seven days, but the first day is the only one mentioned on which the disciples partook of the Lord's Supper (Acts 20:6-12).

In 1 Corinthians 16:1-2, Paul instructed the Christians at Corinth to make contributions on the first day of the week. Don't you think this reference proves it was the custom of the disciples to meet for worship on the first day of the week? I do.

From time immemorial on the first day of the week, Christians have assembled for worship. It is a day of great celebration and rejoicing, the day of the hope of immortality. For multiplied millions it has been and is the day of salvation, comfort, instruction, prayer, fellowship, worship, rest, and service, and—who knows—when Jesus returns to earth, it may be on the first day of the week.

The name "The Lord's Day" comes from Revelation 1:10. In the first section of that glorious book the aged apostle John, said, "I was in the Spirit on the Lord's day." We believe that John was referring to the first day of the week and on that day he received a vision of the victorious Christ.

Jesus did not change the entire meaning of the day, but He gave us a new and different sabbath. He changed the day. As the New Testament says in Hebrews 8:13, since we have "a new covenant, he hath made the first old." When we found ourselves with a new sabbath, we didn't need an old day. Christians are God's people with a new and different day. The old sabbath was buried in the tomb; and with the resurrection of Christ from the grave came a resurrected sabbath, a new sabbath, a different sabbath, the Lord's Day, queen of all days.

With all of my heart I wish that Christians might be careful about how they observe this day. I yearn for them to dedicate themselves anew, letting their observance of the Lord's Day be the declaration that God is God, that Christ His Son died for our sins, was buried, and that He arose from the grave and ever lives.

Will you honor your Heavenly Father by remembering

the commandment to keep this day holy? Will you follow
the example of Jesus by worshiping and doing helpful
deeds? Will you follow the example of John to be in the
Spirit on the Lord's Day?

Leslie D. Weatherhead, London's outstanding preacher during World War II and the postwar years, always
tried to give comfort and to add meaning to people's lives.
He reported, however, a certain failure. He was called to
see a dying man who was past eighty. Dr. Weatherhead
tried, as tenderly as he could, to speak to him about Christian faith. The dying man told him "I have led a very busy
life. I have never had time for that sort of thing." Weatherhead's comment on the experience was this: "But he
had had four thousand Sundays!"

Questions that puzzle you, also puzzle me. People say,
"Jim, you don't go to see the Falcons or Braves play on
Sunday, but don't you watch them on TV? What's the
difference?" Some people ask if it is all right to go out and
eat in a restaurant on Sunday. Some ask about playing golf
on the Lord's Day. What about going in swimming on
Sunday? And, about traveling on Sunday?

No, I do not go to athletic events on Sunday nor do I
watch them on television! Frankly, my Sundays as a minister are always too full for that. Sometimes my work for
Christ compels me to eat out on Sundays and stay in
motels. I do not play golf or go in swimming on Sunday,
but all of these questions trouble me. I believe in the
Lord's Day. I love and honor it. I want to keep it and I try
to keep it the very best I can. I do my best to set a good
example. "If meat make my brother to offend, I will eat
no flesh, while the world standeth, lest I make my brother
to offend" (1 Cor. 8:13).

I am not a Pharisee. But Sunday must be protected and
guarded. There must be some "Thou shalt nots" or else
there will soon be no Sunday for anybody to enjoy. If we

do nothing about it, in two or three generations there will be nothing to take action about. Sunday will be gone and those who call some of us narrow-minded who are trying to observe and preserve Sunday, will see that we are wiser to observe and preserve Sunday, will see that we are wiser than they thought. I respect every person's right to make his or her own moral decision. The main question is not so much what shall I do or not do on Sunday, but how can I honor Christ and observe the Lord's Day in a way that will please Him?

## How Can I Turn My Belief into Action?

Many people ask me to suggest some ways that they may honor Christ on the Lord's Day. I don't want to lay down laws even if I know what is best for them. But after praying about this subject and pondering over it for many years, I would like to conclude by making some suggestions that help me in turning my belief into action.

Begin on Saturday night by studying your Sunday School lesson, getting your clothes ready, preparing your tithe or offering, and by getting a good night's sleep.

Teach respect for the Lord's Day in your home. Keep the Fourth Commandment before your children and interpret it to them in the light of the teachings of Jesus.

Make the Lord's Day a time of happiness for yourself and your family. Give your children and grandchildren positive memories of the day.

Be faithful and regular in your attendance at your church services on Sunday. Sunday is God's gift to us to offer him the worship of our hearts. We are told in Hebrews 10:25 not to forsake "the assembling of ourselves together."

Do not work on this day. Sunday is a day of rest. Unthinking people who demand that this be a day of "business as usual" or a day for entertainment spoil it for others.

Do your shopping during the week. Make no purchases that are not absolutely necessary on Sunday. Encourage merchants to close on Sunday and reward those who close on Sunday by shopping at their stores during the week.

Speak and write letters to editors, legislators, mayors, governors, congressmen, and the president of the United States. Let your voice be heard. Use your influence for the passing of Sunday laws that are constitutional.

Subscribe to *Sunday* magazine. Write The Lord's Day Alliance for a list of available helps and show our movie, *The Lord's Day*. Encourage your pastor to preach on the importance of keeping the Lord's Day and observing it in a manner becoming Christians.

Pray for the proper observance of the Lord's Day for our nation and for The Lord's Day Alliance of the United States.

Sunday is a day for countless opportunites of service. Keep it holy! Never be discouraged and never give up. Sunday is a holy day and should be kept holy all day. It is not a glorified holiday. Sunday is the weekly festival of Christ's resurrection from the grave and should be joyfully and reverently kept as a day of worship, religious instruction, family culture, and humanitarian service.

# 29
# The Significance of Change

by Heather Dau

I'd like to share with you some thoughts about the ways Christians reach out to their communities, how this is changing, and its significance to us in organizations such as The Lord's Day Alliance.

Christians have always been among those who have responded to need and initiated services for the public good. Not that Christians have been alone in this outreach, but it would be an oversight not to recognize the concern, the insights and talents that Christians have contributed to their fellows whether or not those people were Christian.

Motive for this outreach is clearly at the heart of the Christian experience; the divine imperative to "go into all the world"—*all* the world.

That Great Commission has prompted Christians to reach out to their neighborhoods, to their nation, and even to worlds very different from their own. Think of the men and women, born as recently as the 1800s, who set off as missionaries for the heart of China or Angola, Bolivia or India. So strong a motive was again attributed to the New Testament promise that it is out of love for the *world* that God takes on our nature and lives among us.

Through the years, you would find Christians and their churches active in starting schools, hospitals, and literacy programs; in ministering to children, youth, women, and the elderly; establishing services for prisoners, refugees, and immigrants; for native peoples and the handicapped. You'd find them active in the social problems of their day. It continues today.

It's often difficult to recognize what's happening in a situation in which we're part. You remember the story in the New Testament that took place in the Gerasene district, involving a herd of swine? As the swine were racing towards the cliff, one pig was overheard to remark to another: "The main thing is to keep moving and keep together!"

With the distance that history allows, I think social historians and church historians in the twenty-first century will look back on our times and describe a revolution in the making; one they could call a revolution in the helping relationship. It has to do with the relation between the helper and the helpee, and there's evidence of it in both church and society. It's characterized by a change in attitude from one that was formerly *custodial* to one that's increasingly *collegial*. Because churches and Christians have so often seen themselves in the role of custodian-helper, I think it's important to think about what these changes mean to us.

The historians of the future can point back to the 1950s and say, "See how many former colonies became sovereign states?" There was practically an epidemic of new nation-states emerging on the world scene. Along with political independence came church independence. Christian communities begun by early missionaries had come of age. Many were able and eager to stand alongside their parent churches as colleagues and co-workers. It was a time when North American churches were transferring properties and leadership over to Asian and African hands. It was an act of courage and confidence.

Political and church independence required changes

on *both* sides. And those changes from custodial to collegial relationships began influencing, among the churches, mission policies and concepts of ministry that are still being worked out today.

In anticipation for this address, I asked several Canadian church leaders what they thought were the ways Christians reach out and respond differently now than, say, ten-to-twenty years ago. One described it this way: The charitable arm of the churches, those who served in the ambulance crews in Christian social service, have begun looking at the root causes that produce the crises that before they tried to patch up as best they could. They've come to realize their charity, however necessary and well-intentioned, created dependency without correcting the causes. Now they're trying to enable the oppressed to help themselves, rather than bailing them out, but it's requiring changes in attitudes from both the helpers and those helped. It's not an easy transition. It takes time and it's often frustrating.

An example closer to our personal experience: The kind of change that's required is such as occurs between parents and children when the children move away to establish their own autonomy. Again, changes in attitudes and behavior are required on both sides. But when the relationship between parents and grown-up children becomes one of mutuality, we can say a formerly custodial relationship has become a collegial one.

This collegiality is just as much a challenge to institutions and organizations as it is to individuals.

The historians can point back to the 1960s and cite examples of how a number of institutions and bureaucracies set about reforming themselves. The churches started struggling with it. So did hospitals, universities, governments, and business.

It's too soon to say what the outcome of these changes

will be. We're still in the process of experiencing them. However, history may judge our success in terms of how well we learned to relate in a collegial manner.

Naturally, when something new occurs, a few people are in the vanguard of the change, many others are in the rear guard, and most everyone is generally on guard! Church people aren't surprised, as sometimes others are, to find that Christians don't always agree with one another. In fact, it's probably Christians who most often *are* surprised when they do agree! So it won't surprise us then that Christians and their churches will have strongly differing views about this move away from custodial relationships toward collegial ones.

Most of us approach change with a good deal of caution. It's tempting to retreat to familiar and cherished categories and roles when confronted with something unknown. But, in the longer run, I'm convinced the mutuality I've been describing, as between parent and child, will be worth the growing pains we'll all experience.

Just as in the past, Christians have so often pioneered and persevered in service for the common good, I expect the same spirit of courage and outreach from the Christian community today.

Of this movement toward collegiality, what is its significance to us in The Lord's Day Alliance?

First, we who are responsible for planning at a national level may have to develop new ways of relating with regions. The old notion of the pyramid with national as the most important level at the top doesn't reflect mutual interaction. A series of concentric circles would be a better picture of how we want our organizations to work; even the picture of a tree with branches and leaves. Then we can have fun deciding what is the sap that keeps the system thriving!

Those of us charged with administering organizations

need, from time to time, to look at the systems by which we operate to see if they effectively contribute to mutual interaction rather than thwart it. Cooperative federalism is how the Canadian government describes this. But if you know anything about Canadian affairs, you know the Canadians haven't yet struck the golden mean, but we're working on it!

Second, I think collegiality calls for an increased willingness from Christians and their churches to work alongside secular organizations for goals we have in common. That's sometimes easier said than done because there can be misapprehension on both sides. Nonetheless, it happens, so it's not out of the question.

Organizations such as The Lord's Day Alliance represent yet another example of Christian outreach into the community. Let me tell you about the way The Canadian Alliance has reached out and responded.

In 1888, in both Canada and the United States, coincidentally, The Lord's Day Alliance was formed. Canada was only twelve years old, and it was a time before organized labor. The founders of the LDAC, most of whom were Christians, were concerned about the seven-day work week and its effects on the young nation. They wanted a Sunday free from work for sabbath observances. They also expressed concern for the workingman that one day in seven provide relief from commercial and industrial work other than what was called work of necessity and mercy.

Such a purpose brought together members of the LDAC and labor interests to look for solutions. Even in its early years, the Canadian Alliance looked to legislation as the way to ensure Sunday as the day free from unnecessary work. In 1893, John Charlton, an M.P. from Ontario was sent by the LDAC to represent it at the International Conference on Sunday Rest held in Chicago. And by the

early 1900s, the LDAC was mobilizing public opinion to
Prime Minister Wilfred Laurier, urging him to introduce
a federal bill restricting commerce and trade conducted
on Sunday. In it would be spelled out what were exempt-
ed as works of necessity and mercy.

But labor legislation then, as now, was outside the jurisdiction of the federal government. It has always belonged
to the provinces. Religion, however, was within federal
jurisdiction, so the bill that came to be introduced was
called "The Lord's Day Act (Canada)." After much debate, it passed the House of Commons and the Senate in
1906 and became law on March 1, 1907.

The federal politicians were able to satisfy most everyone. Religious and labor interests were satisfied. So were
the provinces by allowing them an opting-out provision.
The opting-out clause was used by the provinces over the
years. They came to enact their own Lord's Day Acts.

Beginning in the late 1960s, the LDAC urged and assist-
ed the provinces to update their Lord's Day Acts. Many
of them had become so out-of-date that provincial attor-
neys general and the police were overlooking their en-
forcement.

Even if religion were within the jurisdiction of the
provinces, I'm sure the LDAC would have agreed with
the provinces that their new legislation belongs to labor
legislation—with regulations about the days and hours of
business. In the province of Ontario, for instance, there
were non-Christian interest groups who wanted new
legislation, but who felt unable to act under the name of
The Lord's Day Alliance. There was formed an ad hoc
committee on Sunday retail selling. That minialliance,
under another name, worked for six years to bring about
the Retail Store Hours Act. It came into effect in 1975, and
Sunday is protected within that act. To date, seven out of
ten provinces have enacted more contemporary laws

about the days and hours commerce and trade can be conducted.

Nor has the federal act remained static. It has undergone four minor amendments, and as recently as 1976, the Law Reform Commission submitted to the federal minister of justice its report and recommendations regarding Sunday observance. One of its chief recommendations was, that after the provinces had had time to update their provincial legislation, that the federal government repeal its Lord's Day Act.

The LDAC, in a brief and delegation to Ottawa, expressed concern that the absence of federal legislation would lead to Balkanization—every province would have a law unto itself, and within provinces, municipalities could opt out. No matter how up-to-date the provincial laws were, it was believed there could be such a patchwork of regulations and enforcements as to become rediculous.

What was an expedient form of legislation in 1906 will inevitably change, and should change. But how it's to be done to realize the public good both regionally and nationally is still an open question.

I think it's a dilemma of conflicting jurisdictions, and not just a problem restricted to the matter of store hours or transporting goods. Offshore oil, broadcasting policy, and pollution of international waters are just some of the other examples of problems within conflicting jurisdictions.

The federal government has been busy with more urgent matters, so the question is still open. I think The Lord's Day Alliance of Canada, with more homework, can develop affirmative guidelines for the federal government that accepts, without fear and trepidation, the practice of decentralized authority.

Now you may feel all this is a long way from what was

envisioned by the founders of LDAC back in the 1880s. That Alliances in differing countries have adopted a variety of ways to achieve their objectives is understandable and desirable.

What we have in common is a religious heritage: that divine imperative to get out into the community and work with others for goals we share. For you and me, it's to encourage our communities and our fellow citizens to reserve Sundays out of the business week as a day of renewal.

Some of us will do this by encouraging ideas, programs, and resources for realizing this goal. Some of us will do it by offering financial support to carry out these plans.

Some of us will be giving encouragement—a timely word or letter that Sunday be a day not like the others.

All of us can be looking for ways to establish and maintain Sunday as a day of renewal.

# 30
# What Sunday Means to Me

by S. Truett Cathy

As a child, Sunday was always a very special day for me. This was the day I dressed up, the best I had, and attended Sunday school and church. This was also the day of no school (hallelujah), and the day my Dad gave me a little of his attention. On Sunday afternoons, we would take a ride in his T-model Ford with my brother to visit aunts, uncles, and cousins.

Starting in the food business in 1946, in a small restaurant we called the Dwarf House, I determined the hours would be twenty-four hours a day, six days a week, thus making the decision to close on Sundays. This was an important decision and a wise decision when you consider the business pressures of a twenty-four-hour operation. The Sunday closing was a reward or relief valve after a demanding week. I do not think I could have stood the pressure day in and day out without this relief and change of pace.

I believe by closing on Sunday we honored God and our attention is directed to more important things. Since we established this position in 1946, we have not varied, but there has been pressure on us to do so. Chick-fil-A, a product concept we originated at the Dwarf House has now expanded to more than three hundred restaurants in thirty-one states, primarily located in shopping malls, and we still have that firm commitment to being closed on Sundays.

Since most of our Chick-fil-A restaurants are located in shopping malls, people who do not know us well assume we're open on Sunday as are the other mall stores. I recently received this letter of apology.

Dear Mr. Cathy:

This is a letter of repentance and apology, though we have never met nor had communications or dealings of any sort. It is occasioned because of my rashness in concluding, and in stating several times to individual and groups of Christians, that there is an inconsistency of witness and deed in your business relationship with Chick-fil-A and your involvement with The Lord's Day Alliance.

I again made that observation last Sunday morning before a Bible class and several members advised me quickly that I am in error, that your restaurants are not open on Sundays as I had believed. (Obviously, I am not one of your regular customers.) I never enjoy being wrong, but in this case I am in a very real sense delighted to know that you have not, as so many of us professed Christians, compromised your convictions on this matter for economic gain.

I thus ask your forgiveness, as I have asked the Lord's, and encourage you in your walk of the Christian way. May you and yours always enjoy the greatest blessings of God's service.

Let Christ be Lord!

Delmar R. Yoder
1583 May Ave., S.E.
Atlanta, Georgia, 30316
(Used by permission)

In dealing with shopping-center leasing agents across the country, we're confronted with our policy of closing on Sunday. The more experienced leasing agents know this is not a debatable issue. In all Chick-fil-A leases, we have permission to close on Sunday. Some of the agents permit us to close on Sunday but only as long as all our restaurants in our chain are closed on Sunday. This is no problem for us.

I received information a few years ago that one of our restaurants in North Carolina was opening on Sunday. I thought the information was not factual because all our operators have a thorough understanding that "closing on Sunday" was a strict policy for the chain. One of our staff people called the restaurant and asked the question, "Are you open on Sunday?" The reply was, "We're open on Sunday during the month of December."

This disturbed me greatly because I was sure the operator understood the rules, and, this particular operator was a part-time music director, he told me, coming aboard, he appreciated the fact of Chick-fil-A closing on Sunday and being able to continue his church music responsibilities.

I suggested to other staff members that we not take drastic action until the daily report sheets were mailed in at the end of the month, to see how he handled his sales report for the Sunday opening; thinking, and even hoping somehow, he misunderstood operating policy. When the sales reports were mailed in, there were no sales reported for Sunday, but the sales were unusually high for Saturday and Monday. (He had divided the Sunday sales and included them on the sales for Saturday and Monday.)

We called the operator and questioned him about the Sunday sales. He admitted that during December he remained open on Sunday because of pressure from mall management and other store tenants—"a spirit of cooperation" was his comment. We were having an incentive contest for sales increases in the month of December, so he was anxious for the incentive awards as well as the added financial awards of additional sales and profit.

We had no other alternative except to terminate our operator agreement with him. The operator's wife called and said that she thought we dealt with her husband too harshly, yet admitted she was shocked when shopping in the mall on Sunday to discover Chick-fil-A was open. Her husband had not shared with his wife his decision to open on Sunday. When principles are violated, many people are affected.

Following is a letter from a shopping-center developer in which he made an attempt to change my policy and also my reply.

Dear Mr. Cathy:

I am the principal owner of (business name). I was born in Knoxville, Tennessee, and started in business in that city. I have been in the building development business for thirty-five years. Our (name of mall) project has almost three million square feet of store space. It is five times the size of an ordinary regional center. We have eight department stores and around three-hundred-fifty individual mall stores. We park twelve thousand cars. We serve a trade area of over one million people.

We are most pleased to have a Chick-fil-A unit in (name of shopping mall).

We have run surveys of people in the mall on Sunday afternoon and we found that almost 100 percent of those who come from church to the center said they came because coming to the mall was recreation for them. We find that people like to mingle in a nice environment and to look at other people. People like to come to places where there are other people and that is low-cost recreation.

As stated, large numbers of well-dressed people come into our mall direct from church. They eat lunch in the mall. They sit on the benches and in our pleasant garden areas. They very much enjoy their visits to the mall. They park free. They pay nothing to come to the mall.

The alternative for these people is to either go home or

to go someplace else other than home. The world has changed from the time I was young, as home was the place where we usually spent our Sundays. However, now most people almost all want to use their Sunday as a holiday. Holiday to most people today means getting out of the house, and mother not cooking. If they go most anyplace else other than the mall—that is, if they go to a movie, a ball game or whatever, it becomes very expensive.

With all the above in mind, we believe is providing a very important public service by being open on Sunday *afternoon.*

I hope I have justified in your mind that it is reasonable and moral for us to be open on Sunday. We do worry about our help working on Sunday, as we know everyone wants to be with their families on Sunday. However, those who work for us on Sunday do so only if they want to do so. We do not require Sunday work. And we believe our employees understand that they are participating with us in providing a public service by being open on Sunday.

We deeply respect your principles which motivate you to want Chick-fil-A to be closed on Sunday. In all our other three-hundred-fifty or so leases, the tenants must be open on Sunday. We accepted your lease because you felt strongly on that issue and we respected you for it. I understand that your main reasons for closing on Sunday are to permit your people to honor the Sabbath and have a day of rest. The purpose of this long letter to you is to call to your attention the following:

1. Our surveys indicate churchgoers are very happy to have us open on Sunday afternoon so they can come here after church at no cost.

2. We reason that it is appropriate for us to ask some of our people to work on Sunday because, by virtue of the need to have a place for thousands of people to come to on Sunday, our mall has become an essential service just as is a drugstore or filling station.

3. Your Chick-fil-A facility employs clean-cut young

people. We have interviewed some of the young people who go to school five days per week and work in other food operations on Saturday and Sunday. Many of these young people work on the weekends to save toward their college education. It is very possible that many of these young people will be able to go to college only if they are permitted to work on Saturdays and Sundays, which are the only days they do not attend school. (Their Sunday workday does not start until after church.)

We would appreciate your giving our letter some deep thought. I ask that you consider opening Sunday afternoons so that Chick-fil-A could fulfill the same function as does (name of shopping mall), that is, provide an essential service for people who want to eat out on Sunday. (Our surveys indicate that a major reason for families eating out on Sunday is so the mother and wife can rest.) We would further suggest that only those who volunteer work on Sunday afternoon.

We would be happy for you to try Sunday afternoon openings and for you to feel free to revert back at any time to closing if you wish.

Your facility is most attractive. You have very tasty products. We have thousands of store employees and Sunday afternoon strollers who are being denied the right to eat in your place on Sunday afternoons. We hope you will give deep consideration to this.

I wish to make it clear that the economic impact on us if you open or stay closed is absolutely minimal. I hope you will think about the fact that there are thousands of families whose only day together is on Sunday and they come to us as family groups. They should have a chance to eat Chick-fil-A products rather than looking through a closed window.

If you feel that the points we set forth in this letter are valid (and you will consider keeping Chick-fil-A open on Sunday,) we would like to offer our contribution in the amount of five thousand dollars to the churches or organizations of your choice.

I would appreciate your advice.

Here is my reply:

Dear Mr._____:

Thank you for your kind and well-worded letter. I'm sure you were speaking your conviction in a generous way and I respect you and what you had to say.

Let me first thank you for permitting us to close on Sunday. We're doing business on your premises and you did not have to make an exception. Because of this, we'll pledge to you exceptional performance during the six days we are open.

Why do we close on Sunday? Well, it all started back in 1946, when I opened my first restaurant, a twenty-four-hour coffee shop called "The Dwarf House." After the first week, I determined that if it took seven days a week to make a living, I should be in some other business. Also, it was my conscience that I had to live with; I just never could come to the idea of dealing with money on the Lord's Day.

I became a Christian at age twelve; not to say that everything I've done since that time is becoming to a Christian, but I believe the Lord has blessed us because of recognizing Him on this special day we call Sunday. Since establishing that policy in the beginning of my business life, we have not varied, and dare not!

If there is any business that is justified in opening on Sunday, I think it is the food business. We eat out often on Sunday after church and find it a great convenience (especially my wife). I do not condemn a business person for opening on Sunday; it is just a principle I stand very firmly on for my business.

Currently, there are more than three hundred locations, all closed on Sunday. Since I don't like to eat at the same place all the time, I say let the people eat some place else on Sunday. We'll feed them during the six days (gives them an appreciation for our food and service).

Mr. (name), you may check us out, but in the vast majority of the malls we are in, we are Number One in sales in food, and in many malls, Number One in sales within the overall tenant mix, even though we do not open on Sunday.

We find closing on Sunday attracts those people who give attention to spiritual growth and are family oriented. The fact that we have Sunday closings helps attract quality housewives and young people as employees. (We offer a one-thousand-dollar scholarship to our young people working two or more years. As of the end of 1985, more than $3 million has been awarded.)

Do you like to work on Sunday? Neither do I, so why should we ask others to do so? We have a bunch of happy people at Chick-fil-A, and we want to keep them that way!

Your thoughts were well received. You are just the kind of person we would like to honor with any reasonable request, but please understand, we cannot compromise on certain principles.

Thank you for including us in your mall and permitting us to remain closed on Sundays. When you are in Atlanta, please come by and give me the opportunity of meeting you personally.

Sincerely,
S. Truett Cathy
President

The Lord set aside one day a week for His day and for man.

Some people have the opinion that equipment works more efficiently and with less breakdowns when given a period of rest. I'm inclined to agree.

Genesis 2:3 says, "And God blessed the seventh day, and sanctified it: because that in it he had rested from all his work which God created and made."

Sunday is a very important day for me and my family, and I find this to be an important day for most people. The nearly eighty-five-hundred crew members of our various Chick-fil-A restaurants appreciate having Sunday off to be with family members, friends, and to worship if they so choose.

I often say, if there is any business that is justified in being open on Sunday, it should be the food-service business. I do not condemn people who open on Sunday because I oftentimes eat out on Sunday, generally after church. But being open on Sunday was just not for me. In speaking to groups, the discussion comes up about Chick-fil-A closing on Sunday, and I tell them that no one likes to eat at the same place seven days a week. "If you'll eat with us six days a week, we'll gladly permit you to eat somewhere else the seventh day." I then add, "Makes you appreciate Chick-fil-A even better. I enjoy eating on Sunday, but never enjoyed washing dirty dishes."

I teach eighth-grade boys in Sunday School at the First Baptist Church, Jonesboro, Georgia. Many times the lesson deals with reverance for the Lord's Day. By closing my business on Sunday, I believe my teaching is more effective, and more believable. It's important that one practices what one preaches.

Chick-fil-A restaurants are located principally in regional shopping malls, and we find the mall trend is moving more and more toward Sunday openings.

But, thanks be unto God, for setting one day aside as a special day, a day for our enjoyment and worship of Him.